Angels in the Kitchen

Body and Soul Food

By Patti Brooks Krumnow

Angels in the Kitchen ♥ *Body and Soul Food*

Copyright © 1998 by Patti Brooks Krumnow

This book contains favorite recipes from my family and various friends. Almost all have been tested and proved the test of time. They should work for you successfully. All diligence has been expended to make sure the ingredients are correct. However, the author has no control over variations in quality of ingredients and oven temperatures, and other factors. Neither Patti Brooks Krumnow, any contributor, publisher, printer, distributor, or seller of this book is responsible for errors or omissions.

ISBN 0-9662967-0-2

Cover Design	Allan C. Kimball and Jennifer Hinnencamp
Book Design	Allan C. Kimball
Interior Art	Jennifer Hinnencamp

Second Edition Published May 1998
BROOKS PUBLISHING COMPANY
P.O. BOX 235
KINGSBURY, TX 78638
830•639•4244

Credits

Thank you all for adding to this effort of love: my cousins, Marci Griffin and her son, Skip. This cookbook reflects the good cooks in part of our family, and all the friends over the years who didn't know their recipes would one day make it to a cookbook.

Dedication

To my three wonderful daughters: Emily Cannell, Dr. Dannette Smith and Claire
Endersby — and Don's daughter, Mandy Krumnow — who have made my life a joy.
This has been a labor of love. It is through this cookbook that my children will share
my memories, and my grandchildren can get to know me and know how much I
loved them all, even before they were born.

• *My daughters Dr. Dannette Smith, Emily Cannell, and Claire Endersby.*

Contents

Foreword

As much as we all need spiritual food, we need good nourishing food which is also good for our souls. You see, I believe we do very little spiritual growing if all our energy is used trying to make financial ends meet. When our basic needs are met for shelter, clothes and food, then we can devote time to our spiritual needs. I've not only shared comforting recipes but some words as well. We, in the South, are born storytellers. Much learning takes place in stories. When we learn to laugh at life's misadventures then we become master's of life. I hope you enjoy some of my family's eccentricities and foibles.

Having grown up in the deep South in a family of outstanding cooks, it would only be natural that I would follow in their footsteps. If not an excellent cook myself, I would at least have a well developed palate. I moved away from home at 20 years old, having shown no interest in learning to cook. However, living with two other girls, all fresh out from under Mama's apron strings, we needed to be able to feed ourselves. My fate was decided when we voted that whosoever cooked did not have to clean up the kitchen. I said, "I do." That started my cooking career with hardly more knowledge than how to boil water. Good recipes saved the day. My mother sent me *The Joy of Cooking* for Christmas, 1960, and with its basic how-to I pulled the cooking experiment off without turning a hair.

We three were flight attendants for Delta Airlines. One of my roommates, Lynn Greer, taught me some very simple lessons like how to clean up as you cook so the kitchen is not a battle zone when you're through. Carole Ann Tessier, my other roommate, taught me the importance of pretty table settings and attractive placement of food on the plate. We were girls in our early 20s but when we sat down to eat, we ate on freshly ironed linen table cloths and napkins and fine sterling silver flatware.

I married a young doctor in 1963. After burning several good meals while waiting for him to come in from the hospital, I learned to cook meals which I could start when I saw the whites of his eyes. My mother told me once that she had never seen anyone be able to walk in the kitchen, with nothing done, and in one hour put a full meal on the table. A lot of the entrees in this cookbook can be prepared very quickly with a minimum of cleanup later.

Along the way, Frank and I had three beautiful daughters, Emily, Dannette, and Claire.

It was after the girls were on their own, calling me for recipes and how-tos, that this cookbook started to take shape. I called friends and relatives and asked for their favorites. I put in all my daughters' favorites which I had cooked over the years. I've contacted cousins to draw on their store of recipes, so this has been a joint effort on everyone's part. The Deep South has become a big melting pot; it is only natural, customs change and food changes. I wanted my daughters who are now living in the Pacific Northwest to have something of their heritage in the way of familiar food. This is not only good Southern cooking, but a little of everything else we loved over the years. I hope you enjoy this as much as I did putting it together.

Blessings,

Patti Brooks Krumnow

• *Carole Ann Tessier, Patti Brooks, and Lynn Greer, circa 1960.*

About the Author

I was born in Montgomery, Alabama, to Annette Horn Brooks and Daniel Jordan Brooks, Jr at Fitts Hill Hospital. My Mother and Daddy drove to Montgomery from Opp for my birth. I am the oldest of three children, followed by Dannette Horn Brooks and Daniel Jordan Brooks, III.

We moved from Opp ("the city of OPPortunity") when I was two years old to Port St. Joe, Florida. I lived a Huck Finn style childhood, surrounded by pine trees, sand dunes, and St. Joe Bay. Those years are the ones that grounded me and gave me a stability that has carried me through a lot of tough times. Those years are ones of very pleasant memories and very personally secure times.

We moved to Montgomery when I was in the fifth grade. I graduated from Sidney Lanier High School in 1957. After attending Rollins College in Winter Park, Florida, the University of Alabama in Tuscaloosa, I finally got my undergraduate degree from Auburn University 31 years later. My degree is in sociology and anthropology. It was easy for me since I had already lived most of the chapters in the sociology books, being a divorced mother of three. Yes, we were the new poverty group, and, yes, there was a time when we qualified for free lunches at school. But the word "broke" has only a temporary meaning for me; we were never poor. We carried our hard times with a certain amount of panache. We called it living in "genteel poverty."

I was a flight attendant in the 1960s for Delta Airlines, and I helped usher in the Jet Age. We were stewardesses back then, when the reputation was still one of glamor. It was before all the flights were full, and you had time to be a genuine hostess and take care of your guests. Few of those flying knew we were actually there for their safety, and were all well-grounded in flight safety and evacuation procedures. I worked in the era of hydraulic failures on the DC-8s, and my roommates and I all had the separate experiences of emergency landings at the nearest Air Force base. This was prior to the Civil Rights Act of 1964, and not only did we have to quit when we got married, we also had to sign a contract that said if we were not married by the time we were 35 years old, we would resign.

I made it until age 23 before I met my intended, a young doctor by the name of Frank E. Smith in Houston, Texas, where I had been sent by Delta. We married in 1963. Over the next six years we had three beautiful girls: Emily, Dannette and Claire. Another fact of the 1970s was divorce, and we got ours in 1974.

I spent the next 17 years as a single parent. I made my living in the field of real estate — managing rentals, sales, and restoring vintage homes. It was this last

• *My husband, Don Krumnow, my first grandchild Brooks Cannell, and me.*

segment that I spent the most time in. I was able to be an at-home mom, but still make a living by redoing the house we were currently living in. We slept on the floor, we lived without kitchens for months at a time. In other words, we all gained an immense amount of flexibility.

When the girls were in junior high school, I got the call to ministry. I wasn't able to fulfill that desire until after they all were through high school, and then Claire, the youngest, and I headed to Missouri to school. Claire to Stephens College and me to Unity School of Religious Studies. I graduated and was ordained in 1990, and headed back to Texas.

I founded the Unity Church in San Marcos, and met and married my soul mate, Don Krumnow. Don had a daughter as well: Mandy, who was 12 at the time. We live in the Hill Country of Central Texas now where Don is a home builder and I am currently serving as minister of the Unity Church of New Braunfels. Emily and Claire are married now and living in the Pacific Northwest. Emily has blessed me with my first grandchild, Brooks Cannell. Dannette is a medical doctor, following in her father's footsteps at Baylor Medical School in Houston. All the girls are doing well. We are all better people for our experiences. My stability still comes from my Alabama roots. These recipes and stories are a reflection of that culture. Read, cook, and enjoy.

God bless you,

Patti Brooks Krumnow

Appetizers

Bird Gravy and Grits

Early on after my divorce from my children's father, I was flat broke. This was one of those times when I couldn't buy a quart of milk. I started looking through the cupboards for what we might eat for supper. I had a date earlier in the week and we had cooked birds from a hunting trip. For some reason I had saved the gravy. Way in the back of the pantry, with a permanent coat of dust that indicated that it had been through many moves, was a little jar (you know the kind — it turns into a juice glass) with dried beef in it. I had bananas and some peanut butter and some grits.

I called the girls to the table. It was set and the plates served. We sat down at our places and as if on cue they all went, "Ughh! What is this?" Well, it was all one color: white. Grits with dried beef in cream gravy, and bananas with peanut butter and mayonaise on top. I just said, "Eat it, girls, it's good for you."

I had a live-in maid briefly at one point, back in the good times, and she asked me one time if I had come from a deprived childhood. Of course, she had come to me from River Oaks in Houston so she had taken a step across the tracks herself. I told her no, that I actually had never done without anything and why on earth would she think that. She said she had never seen a pantry as well stocked as mine. (I was not hoarding. I just detest going to the grocery store so I kept the pantry equipped to the point that I had to go to the grocery only once a month.) Over the months the supply had drastically diminished. But when we needed it, that little bit of food turned into the loaves and fishes .

I have learned over the years that I don't need to get to the point of being backed in the corner before asking for help. And by that I mean ask my Father in prayer. When we ask in prayer, what we are doing is getting our egos out of the way. We admit we can't do it ourselves. For most of us, that is a real difficult admission. When we ask, we have admitted to ourselves that we are helpless. And by that admission of helplessness, we get ourselves out of the way and the power of God is able to come in and work miracles.

Matthew 7:7 — *Ask and it will be given to you; seek and you will find; knock and the door will be opened to you.*

Matthew 7:8 — *For everyone who asks, receives; and the one who seeks, finds; and to the one who knocks, the door will be opened.*

Artichoke Dip

- 1/2 cup Dijon mustard
- 1/4 cup mayonnaise
- 1 Tbls Jane's Krazy Salt or seasoned salt
- 2 12-oz. cans water-packed artichoke hearts,
        drained and chopped
- 2 pkgs cream cheese, softened.

Mix mustard, mayonnaise, salt, and artichokes; add cream cheese and blend well. Microwave 35-40 seconds. Serve warm with chips. Serves at least 16.

Curry Vegetable Dip

- 2 cups mayonnaise
- 1/2 cup sour cream
- 1/2 tsp salt
- 1 Tbls curry powder
- 1/2 tsp garlic salt
- 2 Tsp lemon juice
- 4 tsp sugar
- 1/4 cup parsley minced

Mix all together and serve with fresh vegetables.

Garlic Spinach Dip

- 1 cup mayonnaise
- 1 cup sour cream
- 1 8-oz. can water chestnuts, chopped
- 1 10-oz. package frozen spinach, thawed and drained well
     (squeeze good)
- 1 1-5/8-oz. package dry vegetable soup mix (Knorr)
- 3 cloves garlic, chopped
- 1 large round loaf of bread (sour dough or pumpernickel)
Assorted raw vegetables, plus extra bread for dipping

Mix first six ingredients together for dip. Hollow out the middle of the bread and, immediately before serving, fill with dip. Arrange vegetables and extra bread around loaf.

Tip: dip is better when made the day before serving.

Spinach Dip

- 1 pkg. frozen chopped spinach
- 1 pkg Knorr's vegetable soup mix
- 1 16-oz. carton no-fat sour cream
- 1 cup Mayonnaise
- 1 can chopped water chestnuts
- 2 chopped green onions

Combine soup mix, sour cream and mayonnaise until well blended. Stir in water chestnuts, onions; mix well. Squeeze all the water out of the thawed spinach and mix in last, stirring to blend well. Cover and chill at least two hours. Makes 4 cups.

This is great sandwich mixture on French bread.

Fiesta Dip

- 1 10-1/2-oz. pkg Fritos, crushed
- 1/4 cup butter
- 2 cans 16-oz. refried beans
- 1 pkg taco seasoning
- 1 6-oz. container frozen avocado dip, thawed
- 1 8-oz. container of sour cream
- 3 2-1/4-oz. cans ripe olives
- 2 medium tomatoes, seeded and chopped
- 2 4-1/2-oz. cans chopped green chiles, drained
- 1 8-oz. package Monterrey Jack cheese with peppers, shredded
- 4 Tbls chopped fresh cilantro

Garnish: fresh cilantro sprigs

Combine crushed Fritos and butter; press onto bottom and 2 inches up sides of a lightly greased 9-inch springform pan.

Bake at 350 degrees for 10 minutes. Cool on a wire rack.
Combine refried beans and taco seasoning mix, stirring well; spread over prepared crust. Layer avocado dip and next 6 ingredients over refried beans; cover and chill 8 hours.
Place on a serving plate and remove sides of pan; garnish, if desired.

Serve with large corn chips.

Philly 7-Layer Mexican Dip

- 1 pkg (8 oz.) Philadelphia Brand Neufchatel Cheese
- 1 Tbls taco seasoning mix
- 1 cup each guacamole, salsa and shredded lettuce
- 1 cup (4 oz.) Kraft natural reduced fat shredded
        mild cheddar cheese
- 1/2 cup chopped green onions
- 2 Tbls sliced pitted ripe olives

Mix: cream cheese and seasoning mix.
Spread on bottom of 9 inch pie plate
Layer remaining ingredients over cheese mixture.
Serve with Tortilla chips.

Chopped Chicken Liver

- 1 8-oz. carton chicken livers
- 2 eggs hard boiled
- 2 Tbls grated onion
- 2 dashes Worcestershire
- 2 dashes Tabasco Sauce
- 2 Tbls mayonnaise

Boil chicken livers and 2 eggs in sauce pan with salted water until livers
are done—about 15 minutes. Cool. Grind livers and hard boiled eggs
with a Mouli grater (fine grater). Add rest of ingredients and mix until
spreadable. You might need a little more mayonnaise.

Mound in center of a plate and decorate with ripe olive rings.
Serve with wheat thins.

❦ Annette Brooks

Roasted Garlic Spread

- 1 whole head of garlic
- 1 cup strained yogurt
- 1 Tbls fresh snipped parsley
- 1/4 tsp coarsely ground black pepper
- 1/4 tsp salt

Roast the garlic, then either peel outer skin of each section or squeeze flesh out. You should have a heaping tablespoon. Mix this with the remaining ingredients.

Great with wheat crackers or thinly sliced dark bread.

Seviche

- 2 lbs Halibut
- 2 cups Lemon juice
Marinate 6 hours

Mix in bowl
- 2 cups chopped onions
- 1/2 cup tomato puree
- 1/2 cup tomato juice
- 1 Tbls salt
- 16 green olives chopped
- 2 Tbls Worstershire sauce
- 1 tsp Tabasco
- 2 small green chilis chopped
- 3-4 firm tomatoes seeded and chopped
- 2 Tbls parsley

Cut the Halibut into 1-inch squares and marinate.
Pour off one cup of lemon juice and add all ingredients together overnight.

Fabulous.

Brooks and the Lizard

One Sunday we were all up at the lake. My sister was there with her husband and children. Brooks, her youngest son, was about 10 or 12 years old at the time. He had caught a dark colored lizard in the woods that had spikes on its back and looked for the world like a miniature dinosaur. With that mischievous look on his face he would get real close, and thrust it at me and pull it away. He kept doing this even though I told him to leave me alone; that I was afraid of lizards. He kept right on.

Finally my father, his grandfather, said, "Boy! Did you hear what your aunt said? She's afraid of the lizard. Stop doing that."

Then he gave Brooks one of the most profound lessons I had heard up to that point in my life. Daddy said, "Brooks, if you want a good fight, pick on someone who's your equal. Never pick on a man who's scared of you. A scared man doesn't fight fair — he'll kill you."

Brooks ceased.

I thought a lot about that. When we're in a good spot and everything's going along fine, we rarely get into squabbles with others. We're able to handle any discord with equanimity. But when we're not in a good place and we're already stressed, we come out swinging. We get into our survival mode: our dysfunction. Some of us attack, some of us run for cover, some of us retreat into ourselves and get bulldozed. But we all can think of ways we would have handled it, had we had time to think about it. I have found that if I'm centered — and by that I mean secure and quiet on the inside — I realize that nothing can harm me, this person is not going to physically hurt me in any way and nine times out of ten, it is this person who has the problems. Take the time to assess the situation. Stay quiet and peaceful. Know that this can be worked out. And ask, "How can we solve this problem?"

Proverbs 10:19 — *When words are many, transgression is not lacking, but he who restrains his lips is prudent.*

"Of all the sayings in the world, the one to see you through is, never trouble trouble 'til trouble troubles you."

Oysters Herman

- 2 Tbls melted butter
- 1/4 cup lemon juice
- 1 cup A1 sauce
- 2 Tbls Worchestershire sauce
- 3 Tbls cooking sherry or Madeira wine
- 2 Tbls flour

*Have ready 24 of the best oysters you can find. Roll each oyster sepa-
rately in flour or toss in a paper bag. Lightly butter a pancake griddle or a
heavy skillet and cook the oysters first on one side, then on the other,
until they are lightly browned and just a little crisp. To induce crisping,
sprinkle the oysters with a little melted butter or a few drops of salad oil
while they are cooking.*

*Meanwhile, combine melted butter with lemon juice, A1 sauce,
Worcestershire sauce, and the sherry or wine. Heat thoroughly but do
not allow to come to a boil. Blend flour into 3 Tbls water and stir into the
sauce; cook until thickened.*

*Place the freshly grilled oysters on a hot serving dish. Insert frilled
toothpicks. Surround with the heated sauce. This a rich hors d'oeuvre
and 2-3 should be sufficient for each person. Sauce can be saved,
reheated and used again; and you can also use it as a dip for shrimp.*

❦ Ye Olde College Inn

Pickled Carrots or Okra

Place small okra or carrot strips in jars with a piece of garlic, 2-3 red peppers, dill or dill seed and pinch of alum. Boil 4 1/2 cups water, 3/4 cup vinegar, 1/4 cup salt for 3 quarts or 1/4 cup vinegar, 2 cups water and 1 Tbs salt for 2 pints

Boil vinegar, water & salt and pour over okra and seal. Let stand for 6-8 weeks.

❦ Kay Harrison

Pickled Shrimp
- 1 lb cooked and cleaned shrimp
- 2 tsp olive oil
- 1 cup vinegar
- 2 Tbls water
- 1/4 cup sliced onions
- 8 whole cloves
- 1 bay leaf
- 2 tsp salt
- 1 tsp sugar
- dash cayenne pepper

Dribble oil over shrimp. Bring rest of ingredients to a boil and pour over shrimp and oil while hot. Cool and refrigerate for at least 24 hours.

Pickled Shrimp
- 2 1/2 lbs fresh shrimp

Cook in water, pickling spices,celery tops. Cool.
Layer peeled shrimp and 2 large onions, thinly sliced, add 8 bay leaves.
- 1 1/4 cups salad oil
- 2 1/2 tsp celery seed
- 2 1/2 tsps capers and juice
- 2 tsp salt
- 2 dashes Tabasco

Mix other ingredients and pour over shrimp. Cover container and place in refrigerator for at least 24 hours before serving.

Breads and Grains

And I Am the Bride

Yesterday I was watching *MacMillan and Wife*. At the end of the show the actors were identified and "girl" was played by Elizabeth Lane. Elizabeth Lane is the first cousin of my very best friend in high school, Florence Evans. I began to reminisce about our senior year escapades so much that last night I called Florence in Montgomery, Alabama. She was thrilled to hear from me and so we laughed about our shenanigans for well over an hour. (We had our 40th high school reunion in August, 1997)

Our senior year, second semester, we were feted with graduation parties of all kinds. I had a Hawaiian luau on a Saturday night with all my friends in sarongs and grass skirts. The last few weeks of May consisted of graduation teas. These were parties for the graduate where you got all dressed up — including hat, with or without face veil, and white gloves — and drank punch and ate finger sandwiches. It was at one of these parties that I was introduced to some little round things on crackers with hard boiled eggs on top which I later learned was caviar. Sometimes there were up to six teas in one afternoon, so you went from tea to tea within the allotted time frame.

Florence recalled one of her memories of us that had completely escaped me. This particular afternoon, Florence recalled, the two of us were dressed in our tea finery running late for the tea for Dane Thompson. We were in Florence's '55 red and white Ford convertible (with the top down) flying down Federal Drive when we were pulled over by a motorcycle policeman. Florence was driving and doing the fibbing at this point: "But, Officer, we're on our way to a wedding and we're late." I hopped up and perched myself on top of the front seat in my white dotted Swiss dress with the big puff white sleeves looking for all the world like a redheaded Audrey Hepburn and said, "And I'm the bride!" Whereupon he put on the siren and the flashing blue lights and said, "Follow me," leading us right up to the front door of Dane's house. He waved as we pulled in the driveway and we waved and blew him kisses.

Those were the innocent years of the Fifties with Bobby Darin singing *Splish, Splash, I was Taking a Bath* and *Come Along and Be My Party-Doll*. Where has the fun and humor gone that would allow a young policeman to go along with our charade? We were all happier and more lighthearted as a result.

Lighten up, everybody. This life isn't a dress rehearsal. This is it. Let's enjoy it. As George Bernard Shaw said, "Life is too serious to be taken seriously."

Let us also remember the words of Jesus: *These things I have spoken to you, that your joy may be in you, and that your joy may be full.* **John 15:11**

Corn Pone

- 1 cup corn meal (preferably stone ground)
- 1 tsp salt
- 3/4 cup boiling water
- 1 1/2 Tbls melted fat or shortening

Put corn meal and salt in a bowl and pour the boiling water over it, stirring and blending well. Melt fat in iron skillet or pie pan. You're going to put the pones in this to cook. Pour off the excess fat from the skillet into the mixture. When it is cool enough to handle, shape with your hands into four servings. You pat this with your hands to make it firm—be sure to leave your finger marks in the pone, make it about a half-inch thick. Bake in the pan at 450° a little less than an hour until light brown crust is formed.

You can also fry these in hot fat until golden brown, turn over and cook the other side.

Oatmeal Surprise

- 2 cups quick cooking oatmeal, uncooked
- 1/2 cup chopped dates or chopped dried apples
- 1/3 cup chopped pecans
- 1/2 cup firmly packed brown sugar
- 1 tsp ground cinnamon
- 1/2 cup instant nonfat dry milk powder

Combine all ingredients in a heavy duty zip top plastic bag. To serve, pour boiling water over desired amount of oatmeal mixture, barely covering mixture. Stir and let stand 2 minutes. For thinner oatmeal, add more boiling water, to thicken, add more oatmeal mixture.

Yield: 3 cups oatmeal mix.

Buttery Biscuit Rolls

- 2 sticks butter (no substitute)
- 1 8-oz. carton sour cream
- 2 cups self-rising flour, unsifted

Preheat oven to 350 degrees, melt butter in large saucepan. Add sour cream & flour to butter and mix. Drop batter into miniature, ungreased muffin tin. Fill to top. Bake for 25 minutes.

May be prepared ahead and frozen.
Yield 2 doz.

❦ Margaret Nicrosi Mullen

Banana Bread

- 1/2 cup butter
- 3 crushed bananas
- 2 cups flour, sift then measure
- 1 cup chopped nuts
- 1 cup sugar
- 2 eggs
- 1 tsp soda
- 1 tsp vanilla

Cream butter and sugar; add beaten eggs. Add flour and soda, crushed bananas and mix in. Add nuts and vanilla. Grease loaf pan and line bottom with wax paper. Bake the bread in 350 degree oven for 45 minutes.

English Muffins

- 1/2 cup boiling water
- 3 Tbls shortening
- 2 Tbls sugar
- 1/2 cup evaporated milk
- 1 cake compressed yeast
- 1/4 cup lukewarm water
- 1 egg
- 4 cups sifted flour

Pour the boiling water over shortening, salt and sugar. Add milk. Dissolve yeast in the lukewarm water. Add to milk mixture together with the egg and 2 cups of the flour. Stir until well blended. Add remaining flour and knead in the bowl until firm and elastic. Let rise until doubled in bulk, about 1 hour. Turn dough onto lightly floured board, handling gently to avoid breaking down the bubbles.

Roll out to 1/4-inch thickness. Cut into 4-inch circles. Leave on board and cover. Let rise again until doubled in bulk, about 1 hour. When light, bake slowly on a preheated ungreased heavy griddle or fry pan until browned on the under side about 7 minutes. Turn and brown other side.

Yield 12 4-inch muffins.

Homemade Granola

For about 5 cups:
- 1/4 cup each: oil, honey
- 1/2 tsp almond extract (or 1 tsp vanilla)
- dash salt (optional)
- 3 cups rolled oats
- 1/2 cup wheat germ
- 1/4 cup coarsely chopped nuts
- 1/4 cup bran, sunflower seeds, or sesame seeds, optional
- Dried fruit (raisins, dates, figs, apricots, peaches)

Heat oil, honey, flavoring and salt in a big pot. Stir in all other ingredients, one at a time in the order given, except the dried fruit, which will be added after baking.
Bake at 300 degrees for 15 minutes. Stir. Stir again at 4-5 or 10-minute intervals thereafter until granola barely begins to turn golden. Total baking time about 30 minutes. Do not over bake. Add dried fruit.

Crisp Granola Bars

For about a dozen small squares:
Dry ingredients
- 1 1/2 cups granola
- 1/4 cup whole wheat flour
- 1/4 cup chopped nuts
- 1/4 cup dried fruits
Wet ingredients
- 1/2 cup milk
- 2 Tbls oil
- 2-4 Tbls honey
- 1/4 tsp almond extract or 1/2 tsp vanilla

Combine dry ingredients.
Heat liquids until honey is melted. Mix everything together. Spread on a well-buttered baking sheet about 1/2 inch thick. Score into squares, and bake at 350 degrees for about 20 minutes or until edges begin to brown. Cool completely before serving. Makes about 1 dozen small squares.

Granola Squares

For about 16 squares:
• 1/2 cup oil or butter
• 1/2 cup honey
• 1 egg
• 1 tsp vanilla
• 2 cups granola
• 3/4 cup whole wheat flour
• 1/2 cup chopped nuts or clipped dates
• 1/4 tsp salt
• 1 tsp baking powder

Mix honey with butter or oil. Add other ingredients in the order given, mixing after each addition. Spread mixture about half-inch thick in a well buttered pan, lightly dusted with flour to prevent burning. An 8-inch square pan is ideal. Bake at 350 degrees for 20 minutes until done and edges begin to brown.

Cool before cutting.

Sour Cream Cornbread

• 1 cup self rising cornbread
• 2 eggs
• 8 3/4-oz. cream style corn
• 1 cup sour cream
• 1/2 cup salad oil

Combine all ingredients, mix well. Pour in greased pan (9-inch cake pan will do). Bake at 400 degrees 20-30 min.

Cut in wedges.

Herb Cheese Biscuits

- 2 1/2 cups Bisquick Original Baking Mix
- 1/4 tsp ground white pepper
- 2 Tbls butter or margarine
- 1 cup (4 oz) shredded Swiss cheese
- 4 tsp minced fresh basil
- 4 tsp minced fresh thyme
- 4 tsp minced fresh oregano
- 1 8-oz. carton plain low-fat yogurt

Combine baking mix and pepper in a medium bowl. Cut in butter with a pastry blender until crumbly. Add cheese and herbs, tossing to blend. Stir in yogurt just until dry ingredients are moistened.

Turn dough out onto a surface dusted with baking mix; knead lightly 3-4 times. Roll dough to half-inch thickness, cut with a 2 1/2-inch round cutter, and place on an ungreased baking sheet.

Bake at 450 degrees for 8-10 minutes or until golden. Yield: 1 dozen.

LSU Rolls

- 6 Tbls shortening
- 1 cup warm milk
- 4 Tbls sugar
- 3 1/2 cups flour
- 1 pkg yeast, dissolved in 1/2 cup warm water

In a large bowl, cream sugar and shortening. Add yeast, milk and flour; mix well. Let rise 2 hours. Roll out on floured board to thickness of 1/2 inch. Cut with a biscuit cutter and place on a greased baking sheet. Let rise two more hours. Bake a 400 degrees for 20 minutes or until golden brown.

❦ Marge Zupko

Alabama Hushpuppies

- 2 cups corn meal
- 2 tbls flour
- 1 1/2 tsp baking powder
- 1/2 tsp soda
- 1 tsp salt
- 1 egg
- 3 Tbls chopped onions (you can also add red pepper to taste)
- 1 cup buttermilk

Mix dry ingredients by sifting together. Add onion, milk and beaten egg. Drop by spoonfuls into hot deep fat in which fish has been fried and cook until golden brown.

Skillet Cornbread

- 1 cup yellow cornmeal
- 1/2 cup all purpose flour
- 1/2 tsp salt
- 1 Tbls sugar
- 1 cup buttermilk
- 1/4 cup bacon drippings or melted butter
- 2 large eggs

Grease a 9-inch cast iron skillet; preheat in a 400-degree oven 4 minutes. Combine first five ingredients in a bowl; make a well in center of mixture. Combine buttermilk, bacon drippings, and eggs, stirring well; add to dry ingredients, stirring just until moistened. Pour into hot skillet. Bake at 400 degrees for 20-25 minutes until golden brown. Remove form skillet, and serve warm or at room temperature.

Yield: 6 servings.

Busted

After being home for the weekend from the University of Alabama, I left that Sunday afternoon to return to school. On the way out of town I stopped by Cornelia's house only to find that another good friend of ours was in town from Florida. They had a couple of six-packs and were on their way out of the house. Not being one to turn down the opportunity for a party, I hopped in the back seat of Cornelia's yellow '56 Chevy convertible and off we went.

First we had to go downtown to the old post office and pick up the old man who sat on the steps playing his sweet potato pipe. Cornelia, with aspirations of being a female Hank Williams, never went anywhere without her guitar. (She never made it to Nashville, but she did make it to the governor's mansion with George Wallace.)

So with friends, music and beer we were a moving party. We drove out Narrow Lane Road where there were no people and went down a side road near Allendale Airport. (Allendale Airport wasn't anything more than a stretch of mashed down grass that private planes landed on.) We turned off the dirt road we were on and went down a clearing to a patch of tall pines near a little pond and proceeded to party down. We popped the beers, the sweet potato pipe was making it's melodious harmonica-like sounds and Cornelia was strumming her guitar and we were all singing.

We had just settled in to our private little party when I looked out through the cattails around the pond and thought I saw the top of an egg-shaped bald head. The bald head was holding a rod and reel and doing some serious fishing. I was only 18 years old so I had excellent vision and the more I looked at that head the more familiar it looked. All of a sudden I lost my breath and rasped, "Lets' get out of here... fast." Always alert to sudden danger, Cornelia tossed the guitar in the back seat, cranked the car and started easing out of the trees.

Just as we were about to round the curve out of sight, my Daddy hollered to us: "Bye, girls." Busted.

I found out later, to my complete amazement, that Daddy owned the town's favorite parking grounds.

Mexican Corn Bread

- 1 1/2 cups yellow cornmeal
- 1/2 cup all purpose flour
- 1 Tbls baking powder
- 3/4 tsp salt
- 1 Tbls sugar
- 1 cup skim milk
- 1/4 cup egg substitute
- 3 Tbls margarine, melted
- 1 cup frozen whole kernel corn, thawed
- 1/2 cup (2 oz) shredded reduced-fat sharp cheddar cheese
- 1 4-oz. can chopped green chiles, drained
- 1/2 cup finely chopped onion
- 1/4 cup chopped sweet red pepper
- Vegetable cooking spray

Combine first five ingredients in a large bowl; make a well in center of mixture. Combine milk and next seven ingredients; add to dry ingredients, stirring just until moistened. Pour mixture into a 9-inch square pan coated with cooking spray. Cook at 425 degrees for 25-30 minutes or until golden brown.

Yield: 16 servings.

Mrs. Bryant's Yeast Rolls

- 2 cups luke warm water
- 2 yeast cakes
- 2/3 cups shortening (Crisco)
- 2/3 cups sugar
- 1 tsp salt
- 6 cups sifted flour

Beat well when all ingredients are mixed. Cover with damp dish cloth and let rise. Beat again and put in refrigerator. Pinch off as needed. Knead and shape into rolls and let rise slowly. Bake at 375 degrees for 20 minutes (I'm guessing).

Spiced Tea

- 2 cups Tang
- 1 1/2 cups Instant Tea
- 1 package lemonade
- 1 tsp cloves
- 2 tsp cinnamon
- 1/2 cup sugar

Keeps indefinitely. Keep in a dry place. Do not refrigerate

Southern Biscuits

- 2 1/2 cups sifted, self rising flour
- 1/2 cup lard (or shortening)
- 1 cup buttermilk

Preheat oven to 475 degrees. Lightly grease cookie sheet.

Put flour in large mixing bowl. Make well in center. Add lard and butter-milk. Start working flour into milk and shortening, squeezing mixture through fingers until soft dough is formed. This will be a sticky dough. Lift dough from bowl and place on well-floured surface. Sprinkle a little flour on to top of dough and start folding, gently kneading or pressing with fingertips and turning dough until it is no longer sticky. Pat dough to thinness of about 1/2 inch. Cut with 2 inch biscuit cutter or turn a glass upside down, dip it in flour and use as a cutter. Place on baking sheet.

If you want outside to be crispy, the biscuits should be about 1 inch apart. For a soft biscuit, place with edges touching. Bake for about 8 minutes, until lightly browned. Best served hot from the oven.

Spoon Bread

- 1 cup corn meal
- 1 cup boiling water
- 3 eggs
- 1 tsp salt
- 1 1/2 cups milk
- 1/3 cup melted butter
- 3 tsp baking powder

Pour boiling water over corn meal, stirring to prevent lumping. Beat the eggs well and put them into the milk. Also put salt and baking powder into milk. Add liquid slowly to meal mixture. Mix in melted butter last. Pour into well-buttered casserole and bake at 375 degrees for a little more than half an hour.

Refrigerator Bran Muffins

- 1 15-oz. box Post Raisin Bran
- 3 cups sugar
- 5 cups all purpose flour
- 5 tsp baking soda
- 2 tsp salt
- 4 eggs
- 1 cup vegetable oil
- 1 quart buttermilk
- 2 tsp vanilla extract
- 1 tsp ground cinnamon
- 1 tsp ground cloves
- 1 tsp ground nutmeg

Preheat oven to 400 degrees. Mix dry ingredients in large bowl. Stir remaining ingredients. Mix well. Fill muffin tins 2/3 full. Bake for 20 minutes at 400 degrees.

Batter will last up to 4 weeks in refrigerator.

Mary Jane's Raisin Bran Muffins

- 5 cups flour
- 3 cups sugar
- 2 tsp soda
- 2 tsp salt
- 4 eggs (slightly beaten)
- 1 cup cooking oil
- 1 quart buttermilk
- 1 15-oz. box Raisin Bran (or make these with plain Bran Flakes)

Stir it all up. Grease muffin pans. Bake at 400 degrees about 20 minutes.

Keeps in refrigerator for up to 4 weeks.

Desserts

Change Purse

Back in 1975, about the latter part of June, my ex-husband was coming to pick up the children to spend three weeks with him. This was one of my especially broke times. I figured if I ate a lot of eggs and smoked no more than a half pack of cigarettes a day I could get by for the three weeks until payday.

After he picked up the girls, I headed out the front door and just as I was about to pass through the door I remembered something. I dropped my large shoulder purse on the wooden chair that was sitting just beside the door. As it landed on the chair I heard money — change — and lots of it. I grabbed up the purse and ran my hand all through the bottom of it, but couldn't feel any loose change. I held it by the strap and shook it real good and again I heard the unmistakable jingling of coins. I took it over to the dining room table, removed the contents, and turned the purse upside down and started to shake it again. It responded like a slot machine: nickels, dimes, quarters, half-dollars rolled out everywhere. I was delighted. Money everywhere. I sorted it out and counted it. I had $26. I had a hole in the lining of my purse, and for months loose change had been working its way through the hole so when I dug in the bottom of my purse I couldn't feel it. I was home free. Without the children I could survive. Thank you, God.

Because I have always trusted God so much, these times have not caused panic. But I did finally tell God that I had just as soon not do this 11th hour thing. I was willing to be open to my abundance in an orderly fashion. Over the years, God has proven Himself to me many times; He has a real good track record with me. My children and I have never done without food, shelter or clothing. I know if I practice the spiritual laws, He is always there for me.

And the Lord shall guide thee continually, and satisfy thy soul in drought. . . and thou shalt be like a watered garden, and like a spring of water, whose waters fail not. —
Isaiah 58:11

1949 Brownies

- 1/2 cup butter
- 2 squares chocolate
- 3/4 cup flour
- 1/2 tsp baking powder
- 1/2 tsp salt
- 2 eggs
- 1 cup sugar
- 1 tsp vanilla
- 1 cup chopped nuts

Combine butter and chocolate in a saucepan. Over low heat, melt and then cool (or microwave). Mix together flour, baking powder and salt and set aside. Beat together, eggs and sugar, and add cooled chocolate mixture. Add dry ingredients, and mix well. Pour into greased 8-inch square pan. Bake at 350 degrees for 30 minutes. Cool in pan. Cut into 2 inch square.

❦ Marge Zupko

This classic fudge brownie is so rich it needs no icing. I can't explain the name, except this was the name my mother gave it. — Marge

7-Up Cake

- 1 box yellow cake mix
- 4 eggs
- 3/4 cup cooking oil
- 1 10-oz. bottle 7-Up

Mix ingredients together according to cake mix directions, using only 2 of the eggs in the directions. Then add the remaining eggs, oil and 7-Up. Add this to cake mix. This mixture will be real thin. Bake according to cake mix directions.

❦ Billie Creech Horne

You might prefer to bake this in a flat pan rather than a tube pan like I did.

Frosting for 7-Up Cake
Mix following ingredients: 2 eggs, 1 small can crushed pineapple, 2 heaping tablespoons flour, 1 1/2 cups sugar, 1 stick margarine. Cook in saucepan over low heat stirring constantly until very thick.
Remove from heat and stir in 5-oz. maraschino cherries, drained and chopped, 1/2 cup chopped pecans (more if desired), and1 can or package frozen flaked coconut.
Frost cake. Cut in squares (if baked on flat pan).

Another 7-up Cake

- 3 sticks butter
- 3 cups sugar
- 3 cups flour
- 5 eggs

Cream butter and sugar. Add flour and eggs alternating, one egg at the time. Add 2 tablespoons lemon extract and fold in 3/4 cup 7-up. Bake 325 degrees for 1 hour 25 minutes. Test with cake tester or clean straw from broom. Stick in the middle of the cake. If it comes out clean the cake is done. Be sure to do this before you take it out of the oven. If there is a variation in the temperature in your oven it might not be done. When you take it out it will fall flat and you will have lemon pudding. Let it cool; then ice.

Icing
- 1 1/2 cups powdered sugar
- 1 tsp lemon zest
    Zest is when you run the lemon over a fine grater. Those little threads are the zest.
- 3 Tbls lemon juice
- 1 Tbls extra virgin olive oil.

Combine all the ingredients and drizzle over the cake.

❦ Sara Brooks

Apple Cream Pie

- 2 12-oz. packages Stouffer's escalloped apples, thawed
- 1 tsp cinnamon
- 2 tsp lemon juice
- 1 cup marshmallow cream
- 1 8-oz. package cream cheese, softened
- 1 unbaked 9-inch pastry shell
- 2 Tbls light brown sugar
- 1/4 cup all purpose flour
- 2 Tbls butter or margarine
- 1/4 cup chopped walnuts
- 1/2 cup powdered sugar
- 1 Tbls water
- 1/2 tsp vanilla extract

Combine first three ingredients in a medium bowl, stirring well. Beat marshmallow cream and cream cheese at medium speed with an electric mixer until well blended; fold into apple mixture, spoon into pastry shell; place on a baking sheet.

Combine brown sugar and flour; cut in butter wih a pastry blender. Stir in walnuts; sprinkle over apple mixture.

Bake at 375 degrees for 40 to 50 minutes. Combine powdered sugar, water and vanilla, stirring well; drizzle over warm pie.

Serve at room temperature or chilled.

Quick Apple Dessert

- 1 cup sugar
- 1/4 cup butter
- 2 eggs, beaten
- 2-3 apples, peeled and grated
- 1 cup all purpose flour
- 1/2 tsp salt
- 1 tsp soda
- 1 tsp ground nutmeg
- 1/2 tsp ground cinnamon
- sauce (see below)

Cream sugar and butter until light and fluffy; add eggs and beat well. Stir in apples. Combine flour, salt, soda, nutmeg, and cinnamon; add to apple mixture and stir well. Put into a lightly greased 9-inch glass pie pan. Bake at 350 degrees for 50 minutes. Serve warm or cold with sauce.

Serves eight.

Sauce
- 1 cup sugar
- 1/2 cup half-and-half
- 1/2 cup butter
- 1 1/2 tsp vanilla or bourbon

Combine ingredients in a saucepan. Cook over low heat, stirring until sugar is dissolved.

Makes one cup.

Apple Pan Dowdy

- 1 1-lb 4-oz. can sliced apples
- 1/2 tsp cinnamon
- 1 Tbls sugar
- 1 Tbls butter
- Bisquick shortcake dough rolled 1/2-inch thick

Turn apples into a casserole. Sprinkle cinnamon and sugar over the apples, and dot with butter. Cover with Bisquick dough and bake at 450 degrees for 15-20 minutes. Serve hot with hard sauce.

Serves 4.

Hard Sauce
- 1 cup confectioner's sugar
- 2-5 Tbls butter
- 1/8 tsp salt
- 1 tsp vanilla, coffee, rum, whisky, brandy, lemon or orange juice
- 1 egg or 1/4 cup cream

Cream the softened butter in a small bowl at high speed. Add the sugar gradually. Add the flavoring. Beat the sauce until it is creamy, about 5 minutes. Scrape the sides of the bowl once or twice while beating. Chill the sauce.

Apple Dapple Cake

- 3 eggs
- 1 1/2 cup salad oil
- 2 cups sugar
- 3 cups all purpose flour
- 1 tsp salt
- 1 tsp soda
- 2 tsp vanilla
- 3 cups chopped apples
         (or two mashed bananas: take the black ones out of the freezer*)
- 1 1/2 cups chopped pecans
- topping (see below)

Mix eggs, salad oil and sugar and blend well. Sift flour, salt and soda; add to egg mixture, add vanilla, chopped apples and nuts. Pour into a greased 8-9-inch tube pan, Bake at 350 degrees for 1 hour or until straw comes out clean. While cake is still hot, pour hot topping over it in the pan and let cool. When completely cool, remove from pan.

Topping
- 1 cup brown sugar
- 1/4 cup milk
- 1 stick margarine

Combine all ingredients and cook 2 1/2 minutes. Pour Immediately over cake in pan.

* The girls and I have a running joke about the bananas I save by putting them in the freezer when they get a little too ripe. Freezing causes them to turn black but it doesn't hurt them.
You can substutute bananas for the apples and make fabulous banana cake.

Creek and Snakes

Several years ago a memory surfaced that I was rather puzzled about. I thought perhaps it had been a childhood dream, but the more I thought about it the more I thought it had really happened, otherwise it would have been remembered as a nightmare of the worst kind.

The setting was beautiful — one of those shady wide creeks in or near the Dead Lakes of northern Florida. My Daddy, grandfather and I were in a small flat-bottomed boat, a man at each end and me, a child of about four years old, in the middle. As I sat there I observed what was going on. The water moccasins were so thick they looked like hundreds of hands with fingers sticking up out of the water. They were swimming towards the boat and some were trying to slide into it. My Daddy, on the front seat of the boat, was beating them off the bow of the boat with a paddle. My grandfather at the other end was shooting them with a pistol. I watched this display with much interest. I recall no feelings of fear just interest and excitement.

When I went to Montgomery a few months after this memory surfaced I remembered to ask my Daddy if he remembered the event. "I sure do," he said. "We had caught a big string of bream and Daddy Rue and I were cleaning them in the boat and throwing the entrails overboard. This attracted the moccasins from everywhere. That was quite a sight."

Now knowing the full story, I really gave my feelings about this scenario a good deal of thought. I felt no fear. I realized that I had such a deep trust in these two important men in my life, that I had no reason to fear. I knew with all my heart with these two men looking after me, nothing could harm me. What pure trust.

As an adult, I have actively sought to trust God with as much trust as I had for my father. You see, trust is a choice. It is a decision you make. Everyday I turn my life over to God, trusting Him to lead me in the way he wants me to go. With His leading, I know I will be safe. Even when appearances seem to be to the contrary there is that deep peace that I call the calm peace of my soul. Outside of me there may be lots of confusion and activity but deep inside there is peace and quiet. Yes, I do trust my Father, God.

Psalms 4:8 — *In peace I will both lie down and sleep; for thou alone, O Lord, makest me dwell in safety.*

Aunt Lina's Cherry Ice Cream

- 3/4 cup sugar
- 1 Tbls lemon juice
- 1 cup evaporated milk
- 1 cup heavy cream (whipping cream)
- 2 small jars of cherries (I think juice, too)

Mix sugar, lemon juice, let stand until sugar melts (about 20 mins). Add milk and slightly whipped cream. Pour into freezing (ice) tray. When frozen, remove from tray and beat until smooth. Return to tray and refreeze.

Serves 6.

❦ Lina Creech Bouton
> *Also known as Nina, mother of William (Bill) Bouton.*
> *Aunt Nina was Grandmother Horn's sister.*

Baked Custard

- 4 eggs, slightly beaten
- 1/2 cup sugar
- 1/4 tsp salt
- 3 cups milk, scalded
- 1 1/2 tsp vanilla extract
- ground nutmeg

Combine eggs, sugar, and salt and stir until well blended. Slowly pour milk into egg mixture, stirring constantly. Add vanilla. Pour into six 5-ounce custard cups or a 1 1/2 quart casserole. Sprinkle with nutmeg. Set in a large baking pan and pour hot water into pan to within 1/2 inch of top of custard. Bake at 325 degrees until a knife inserted halfway between center and outside edge comes out clean (35-40 minutes for individual cups and 45-50 minutes for casserole.) Remove promptly from hot water. Serve warm or chilled.

Yield: 6 servings

New Orleans Bread Pudding

- 1 10-oz loaf French bread, broken into pieces
- 4 cups milk
- 2 cups sugar
- 1 stick butter, melted
- 3 eggs
- 2 Tbls vanilla
- 1 cup raisins
- 1 cup coconut
- 1 cup chopped pecans
- 1 tsp cinnamon
- 1/2 tsp nutmeg

Combine all ingredients; mixture should be very moist, but not soupy. Pour into buttered baking dish. Place on middle rack of oven. Cook at 350 degrees for about 1 hour 15 minutes until top is golden brown. Serve with the sauce of your choice: whiskey or lemon.

☙ Marge Zupko

Lemon Sauce
- 4 egg yolks
- 1/2 cup sugar
- 4 Tbls flour
- 1 1/2 cups milk, scalded
- 4 Tbls lemon juice

Beat yolks slightly; add sugar and flour. Gradually pour into scalded milk, Cook over low heat until thick. Remove and add lemon juice.

Yield: 8 servings.

Bread Pudding

- 1 cup milk
- 1/4 cup sugar
- 1 Tbls melted butter
- 1 egg, slightly beaten
- 2-3 slices crumbled bread
- 1/8 tsp cinnamon
- 1/8 tsp nutmeg
- 1/4 cup seedless raisins
- 1/4 tsp lemon peel

Combine all ingredients and pour into custard cups; set in a pan of water. Bake at 350 degrees for 40-45 minutes.

Makes two servings

Peach Blueberry Crisp

- 6 cups peeled sliced fresh peaches
- 2 cups blueberries
- 1/3 cup brown sugar packed
- 2 Tbls flour
- 2 tsp cinnamon

Topping
- 1 cup rolled oats
- 1 tsp cinnamon
- 1/4 cup brown sugar-packed
- 3 Tbls soft butter

In an 8-cup baking dish combine blueberries and peaches. In a small bowl combine sugar, flour, and cinnamon. Add to fruit and toss to mix. Combine oats, sugar and cinnamon. With pastry blender, cut in butter until crumbly. Sprinkle over top of fruit mixture. Bake in preheated 350 degree oven for 25 minutes until mixture is bubbling and fruit is barely tender.

❦ Marci Griffin

Banana Cake

- 1 stick butter
- 1 cup sugar
- 1 1/2 cups flour
- 4 Tbls butter milk
- 2 large ripe bananas, mashed
- 1 egg
- 1 tsp soda
- 1/4 tsp salt
- 1 tsp vanilla

Cream butter, add sugar, cream well. Add bananas and egg. Mix soda in buttermilk. Add vanilla. Fold in flour and salt.

Ice with butter rum icing or serve in squares with whipped cream. May also serve as small oblong cakes rolled in powdered sugar.

🌱 Christine Griffin
Joe Griffin's sister who is married to Marci Dillon Griffin.

Annette's Dutch Cheese Wafers

- 1 3-oz. pkg cream cheese
- 1 cup flour
- 1/2 cup butter
- 1/2 cup sugar
- dried fruit

Thoroughly blend cheese, butter, sugar and flour. Shape in long rolls one inch in diameter. Wrap in wax paper and chill over night. Slice thin with sharp knife. Place piece of dried fruit in center, cover with another slice, press together. Brush top of cookies with milk. Sprinkle with sugar and bake in moderate oven 350 degrees for about 7 minutes.

🌱 Annette Brooks (Patti's mother)

I remember these from being a little girl in the 1940s.

Banana Nut Spice Cake

6 Large ripe bananas
1/2 cup vegetable oil
1/4 lb butter
• 2 cups sugar
• 4 eggs
• 3 cups flour
• 2 tsp soda
• 2 1/2 tsp cinnamon
• 1 1/2 tsp ground cloves
• 1/2 tsp salt
• 1 1/2 cups seedless raisins
• 1 1/2 cups chopped pecans

Mash bananas; pour vegetable oil over bananas and let stand while mixing cake. Cream butter and sugar; add eggs, one at a time, beating well after each addition. Stir in banana mixture and mix well. Add dry ingredients which have been combined. Stir in raisins and pecans and mix thoroughly. Spoon mixture into three greased loaf pans and bake at 250 degrees for 1 1/2 hours.

Bon Bons

• 1 cup butter
• 1 1/2 cup confectioners sugar
• 1 well beaten egg
• 1/2 tsp vanilla
• 1/2 tsp almond extract
• 2 1/2 cups flour
• 1 tsp soda

Thoroughly cream butter and sugar, add egg and flavorings. Add dry ingredients and cool one hour. Roll in small balls, mash and put almond on top. Bake at 375 degrees for about 12 minutes.

❤ Annette Brooks

Carrot Cake

- 4 eggs
- 2 tsp soda
- 2 cups sugar
- 2 tsp cinnamon
- 1 1/4 cup salad oil
- 3 cups coarse grated carrots
- 2 cup flour
- 2 tsp baking powder

Beat eggs; add sugar, oil and sifted dry ingredients. Add carrots, stir nuts in last. Pour into three greased 9-inch cake pans. Bake in 325-degree oven for 25 minutes.

Frosting
- 1 pkg. cream cheese
- 1 box confectioner's sugar
- 1 stick butter
- 1/2 cup nuts
- 1 tsp vanilla

Cream all ingredients together. Spread between layers and over cake. This cake is better the second day. Keep refrigerated.

You can substitute zucchini, or pumpkin.

❦ LaRue Jolly

Chess Cake Squares

These cookie squares resemble a brown sugar chess pie. They have a cookie crust and transparent filling that literally melts in the mouth. No other dessert is necessary.

- 3/4 cup butter
- 1 1/2 cups sifted flour
- 3 Tbls sugar
- 1/2 tsp vanilla
- 2 1/4 cups dark brown sugar
- 3 egg yolks
- 1 cup coarsely chopped pecans
- 3 egg whites

Cream butter. Add slowly the sifted flour and sugar. Pat into a long rectangular biscuit pan with 1 1/2-inch sides, and bake 20-30 minutes in 375-degree oven or until crust is golden brown. Meanwhile make the filling by mixing the dark brown sugar with the beaten egg yolks. When thick and spongy add the pecans. Add vanilla; fold in the stiffly beaten whites. Spread filling evenly on the crust. Return pan to oven and cook 25-30 minutes longer or until the filling sets. Do not cook too long as the filling should be transparent and semisoft. Dust with powdered sugar and when cool cut into 1 1/2 inch squares.

🍎 Miss Bertha Kahn

Daddy's Dog Shep

When I lived in Montgomery, Daddy and I got together frequently. We often had lunch together and, oddly enough, we were so much alike that we would get hooked on a certain menu like Szechuan pork and we would eat it everyday for three or four weeks.

It was one of those times that out of the blue he said, "You know I always hated Sheriff Duff for killing my dog. Shep and I had been companions since as early as I could remember." (In fact, there is a lovely portrait of Daddy at about four years old with Shep sitting beside him with Daddy's arm around his neck.) But he continued by saying, "You know, we had a rabies epidemic in Elba and he had to kill my dog." Almost 70 years had passed since that event and all these years Daddy had felt that most dreadful feeling. But as a small boy of five he couldn't possibly comprehend what a rabies epidemic meant before vaccines, and what deadly consequences it could have for his small home town. But in that moment of mature clarity his perception of the death of his dog and Sheriff Duff suddenly changed. He understood at that moment how difficult but necessary Sheriff Duff's job had been. Forgiveness came.

Over the next few months I watched that process happen over and over. I knew in my heart of hearts that Daddy was being given all the opportunity he needed to practice forgiveness and get his own slate clean. What a loving, merciful God we have who loves us enough to churn our memories for us. With just a slight turn He puts an event in a different perspective so we might view another side, thus allowing us to see the big picture. In the case of Shep, this new view brought an understanding that through the eyes of a child could have only meant utmost cruelty.

I have found this is the way forgiveness works in my own life. First, I must be willing to give up my feelings of anger, betrayal or resentments. Then I must become willing to forgive. God works the process through me and then one day, one moment, I realize that forgiveness has taken place and in that agitated, upsetting place of unforgiveness is peace, understanding and compassion.

Judge not according to appearance, but judge righteous judgment. — **John 7:24**

And the Lord direct your hearts into the love of God, and into the patient waiting for Christ. — **II Thessalonians 3:5**

Chocolate Cake

- 2 cups all-purpose flour
- 1 1/2 cups Domino chocolate flavored confectioner's sugar
- 1 cup water
- 3/4 cup butter or margarine, softened
- 3 large eggs
- 1 1/2 tsp vanilla extract
- 1 tsp baking soda
- 1/2 tsp baking powder
- 1/2 tsp salt
- chocolate sour cream frosting (see below)

Beat first nine ingredients at low speed with an electric mixer just until blended. Beat at high speed 3 minutes. Pour into 2 greased and floured 8 inch round pans.

Bake at 350 degrees for 25 minutes or until a wooden pick inserted in center comes out clean. Cool layers in pans on wire racks 10 minutes; remove from pans, and cool on wire racks.

Spread chocolate frosting evenly between layers and on top and sides of cake.

Chocolate Sour Cream Frosting
- 1 16-oz. package Domino chocolate flavored confectioner's sugar
- 1/2 cup butter or margarine, softened
- 1/2 cup sour cream

Beat all ingredients at medium speed with an electric mixer until smooth. Makes 4 cups.

Chocolate Fondue

In the top of a double boiler, melt one package (6 ounces) semisweet chocolate morsels over hot (not boiling) water. Blend in 1/3 cup orange juice. Cut a 10 3/4-ounce pound cake into 36 1-inch-square cubes for dipping into chocolate sauce.

You can also dip fruit pieces, marshmallows or pretzels.

Pour chocolate mixture into a small serving bowl or a fondue pot.

Serves four to six.

❤ Marci Griffin

Chocolate-Raspberry Cheesecake

- 1 cup low-fat cottage cheese
- 1 cup sugar
- 1 8-oz. lite cream cheese
- 1/3 cup cocoa powder
- 3 Tbls raspberry liqueur
- 1 tsp vanilla extract

Whip above ingredients in blender or food processor. Place mixture in a bowl and add 3 tablespoons egg beaters, 3 tablespoons semi-sweet chocolate chips. Pour in cheese cake spring form pan. Bake at 300 degrees for 35-40 minutes.

Juanita Krumnow

Egg Custard Pie

You start with a neatly crimped, 9-inch pie shell, unbaked. Be sure there are no bubbles under the pastry and no holes in the pastry. Let the pie shell chill while you're making the filling. That's custard pie, plain and simple. Don't cut a custard pie until you're ready to serve it.

Filling
Blend 4 eggs, slightly beaten, 1/2 cup sugar, 1/4 tsp salt, 1/2 tsp vanilla and 1/2 tsp almond extract. Gradually stir in 2 1/2 cups scalded milk. To avoid any oven spills, add the last cup of filling just before you close the oven door.

Variations
Almond Custard — Brown 1 cup chopped blanched almonds in 2 Tbls butter in the oven. Sprinkle over bottom of pastry.

Butter Custard — Add 2 Tbls butter to milk before scalding. This makes a nicely browned top in finished pie.

Coconut Custard — Sprinkle 1 cup finely cut shredded coconut over pastry; pour custard over.

Graham Cracker Custar — Roll over plain pastry; sprinkle with 1/3 cup fine graham cracker crumbs. Roll crumbs lightly into crust. Place pastry in pan, crumb side down.

Fresh Coconut Cake

Cake layers
• 1 stick butter
• 1/2 cup shortening
• 2 cups sugar
• 3 egg yolks
• 3 cups all purpose flour
>   *I always used unbleached flour; you at least get some nutrition*
>   *with the calories.*
• 1 Tbls baking powder
• 1/4 tsp salt
• 1 cup milk
• 1 1/4 tsp vanilla extract or almond flavoring
• 5 egg whites

Preheat oven to 350 degrees. Grease and flour three 9 inch cake pans.
In large bowl, cream together butter, shortening and sugar. Add egg
yolks, one at at time, greasing well after each addition. In medium bowl,
combine flour, baking powder and salt. Stir to mix. Add flour mixture to
creamed mixture alternately with milk, starting and ending with flour. Add
vanilla, mix well. Beat the egg whites until stiff peaks form. Fold into
batter. Divide batter evenly among prepared pans. Bake for 20-25
minutes or until wooden pick comes out clean when inserted in center of
layers. Remove from pans immediately and cool completely on racks
before frosting.

For frosting, see next page.

Coconut Frosting

- 2 egg whites
- 2 tsp light corn syrup
- 1 1/2 cups sugar
- 1/3 liquid drained from fresh coconut
- 1 tsp vanilla extract
- 1 fresh coconut, peeled and grated (about 3 1/2 cups)
    *Make it easy on yourself and buy canned grated coconut and
    leave out the sugar; and buy canned coconut milk for the liquid.*

*Combine egg whites, corn syrup, sugar and coconut in top of double
boiler. Beat with electric mixer for about 1 minute, until well mixed. Place
over boiling water. Cook for 7 minutes, beating continuously with electric
mixer. Frosting should be thick and glossy. Remove from heat and stir in
vanilla.*

*Spread frosting on one cooled cake layer and sprinkle generously with
grated coconut. Repeat with second and third layers. Spread frosting
around sides of cake and cover with coconut.*

Easy Fruit Cobbler

- 1 pkg. Duncan Hines yellow cake mix
- 1 stick butter or margarine
- 1 can pie fruit (cherries, apple, peach, blueberries)

Pour fruit in bottom of 2-quart Pyrex dish. Sprinkle with half box of cake mix. Top with pats of butter evenly over the top. Bake at 350 degrees for about 30-40-minutes until golden brown and bubbly.

Variations
Use spiced cake mix with apples.
Top cherry with slivered almonds.

Serve topped with Cool Whip or ice cream.

Cream Candy

- 2 cups sugar
- 1/2 cup top milk (I think this means cream)
- 1 tsp vanilla
- 1 cup pecans

Mix milk and sugar and stir until it boils; boil 5 minutes without stirring. Remove from fire and set saucepan in cold water, beat until it gets creamy, then add nuts and vanilla. Pour into 8 x 8 pan until set. Slice into squares.

This is my Grandmother Brooks' recipe.

French Apple Bread Pudding

- 3 eggs
- 1 can condensed milk
- 2 cups apples, peeled and chopped fine
- 1 3/4 cup hot water
- 1/4 cup butter, melted
- 1 tsp cinnamon
- 1 tsp vanilla
- 4 cups French bread cubes
- 1/2 cup raisins
- whipped cream or Cool Whip

Preheat oven to 350 degrees. Beat eggs, add condensed milk, apples, water, butter, vanilla and cinnamon. Stir in bread and raisins. Turn into buttered 9-inch baking dish. Bake 1 hour or until firm. Cool. Serve warm with cream or Cool Whip.

Grand Daddy's Divinity

- 2 cups sugar
- 2 tsp vanilla
- 2/3 cup light corn syrup
- 1 cup walnut or pecans
- 1/2 cup water
- 2 stiffly beaten egg whites
- 1/8 tsp salt

Combine sugar, corn syrup, and water; stir over low heat until sugar dissolves. Cook to light crack stage (270 degrees). Slowly pour over egg whites, beating constantly with slotted spoon or rotary beater. Add vanilla. Beat until mixture holds its shape. Add nut meats. Drop from teaspoon onto greased pan or waxed paper. If desired, spread in greased pan; cool and cut in squares. One half cup chopped, candied cherries may be added with nut meats (but not in Grand Daddy's). Makes 3 dozen pieces.

❦ Dan J. Brooks, Jr.
   My daddy.

Dannette's Tangled Hair

My sister and I had our tonsils out when we were quite young. I was about five, she was about three. I don't remember much discomfort with the surgery, but I do remember that we got to eat all of the ice cream we wanted.

Dannette had complications. She hemorrhaged and had to go back to the hospital for observation. Surgery and all added up to several days. My next memory was of being in Elba at Grandmama Brooks' house. I don't know how much time had transpired since our tonsillectomies, I hope not long.

Dannette was extremely tender-headed and had not let anyone comb her hair since before the surgery. Remember, she has been bedridden for some days after surgery and hemorrhage. Not a pretty sight. Grandmama will always be the closest thing to a saint I'll ever know. She sat Dannette down on a stool in front of her and started telling her stories, and starting at the very base of her neck hair she started combing little bits at a time. Holding the hair close to the roots, she started at the very ends of the hair and worked up towards the scalp a little at the time coaxing the tangles to give up their fierce hold. This process must have taken hours, but Dannette finally had a shampoo and clean straight shiny hair again.

And I learned how to comb a little girl's hair so when I had three little girls of my own 20 years later I knew a painless way to deal with tangles.

Dannette's Coconut Pie

- 1 pie shell, cooked
- 1/4 cup, plus 2 Tbls cornstarch
- salt (less than 1/8 tsp, about the size of flat dime in your hand)
- 1 cup sugar
- 2 cups milk (at least 2 percent)
- 3 eggs separated
- 1 Tbls butter
- 1 tsp vanilla
- 1 1/2 cups coconut (canned angel flake, not frozen)

Be cooking pie crust according to directions. Stir dry ingredients together in 2-quart saucepan. Add 1/4 cup milk to dry mixture and stir until well blended and not lumpy. Reserve 1/4 cup of milk to add to egg yolks. Then add the rest of the milk and stir well. Separate eggs and beat yolks. Add 1/4 cup milk to yolks. Heat sugar and milk mixture over medium heat until it begins to thicken. Remove 3 tablespoons heated milk and add to set aside yolks. Slowly pour yolks into hot custard mixture, stirring constantly until thickened. Be careful not to scorch. Stir until liquid is absorbed. If it's lumpy, do not worry. When you add the butter you will be able to stir the lumps out. Remove from heat and stir in butter and vanilla. Let cool briefly and then add coconut and stir.

Always pour warm cream pie filling into a warm crust.

Beat egg whites until stiff and add 4 tablespoons sugar. Cover pie with whites (meringue) and be sure the edges are sealed. Sprinkle top of pie meringue with about 1 Tbls loose coconut. Bake at 350 degrees until meringue is golden, about 10 minutes.

Aunt Netta says, "If you don't have egg whites all over the kitchen when the pie goes in the oven, you didn't do it right."

❦ Dannette Brooks

Date Nut Refrigerator Cookies

- 1/2 stick butter
- 1 cup brown sugar
- 1/2 tsp vanilla
- 1 egg unbeaten
- 1 1/4 cup flour
- 1/2 tsp soda
- 1/2 tsp cream of tartar
- 1/8 tsp salt
- 1/2 tsp cinnamon
- 1/4 cup chopped dates (dust with flour)
- 1/4 cup chopped nuts

Combine butter, sugar, and egg. Beat till light and fluffy. Stir in dates and nuts. Shape into long roll about 1 1/2 inches in diameter. Wrap in foil or freezer paper. Chill in refrigerator over night. Slice thin and bake on greased cookie sheet in 375 degree oven for 7-10 minutes. Makes about 4 dozen cookies.

Dough can be frozen 3-4 months.

Date Pudding

- 1 cup all purpose flour
- 2/3 cup sugar
- 1 1/2 tsp baking powder
- 1/4 tsp salt
- 1/2 cup milk
- 1 cup chopped dates
- 3/4 cup firmly packed brown sugar
- 1 1/2 cups water
- 1/4 cup butter
- whipped cream (optional)

Combine flour, sugar, baking powder, and salt; mix well. Add milk, mixing well. Stir in dates. Spread batter in a greased 10 x 6 x 1 3/4-inch pan. Combine brown sugar, water and butter in a saucepan; bring to a boil. Boil for 2 minutes. Pour over batter and bake at 350 degrees for 30-40 minutes. Garnish with whipped cream. Serves six.

Date Nut Cookies

- 2 tsp sugar
- 2 cups chopped dates
- 1/2 cup boiling water
- 1 cup butter
- 1 1/2 cups sugar
- 2 eggs, beaten
- 1 cup coconut or raisins
- 1 cup chopped nuts
- 1 tsp vanilla
- 3 1/4 cups flour

Sprinkle soda over chopped dates. Add boiling water, stir well, and set aside. Cream butter and sugar; add eggs and beat well. Stir in dates, coconut, nuts, and vanilla and mix well. Add flour and mix well (batter will be very stiff). Drop by teaspoonfuls onto greased cookie sheets and bake at 375 degrees for about 12 minutes or until browned.

Yield: about 7 dozen.

Datenut Cake

- 1 lb dates
- 1 qt pecans
- 1 cup flour
- 1 cup sugar
- 2 tsp baking powder
- 2 tsp vanilla
- 4 eggs separated
- 1 tsp salt

Cut dates, add to flour. Toss well. Mix sugar, salt, baking powder, and chopped nuts. Mix in dates and flour. Separate eggs, set whites aside. Beat yolks and mix into dry ingredients, add vanilla. Beat egg whites until stiff. Fold into mixture until moistened. Bake at 300 degrees for 50 minutes to1 hour.

❦ Dan J. Brooks
> *A traditional Christmas cake for us, along with his Divinity.*

Deep Dish Apple Pie

- 3 12 oz packages frozen escalloped apples
- 1/4 tsp nutmeg
- 4 tsp lemon rind
- 4 tsp lemon juice
- 4 Tbls melted butter
- pastry for 9-inch pie

Place the apples in microwave to defrost. Remove and add the other ingredients. Blend thoroughly and place in deep baking dish. Cover the dish with the pastry, flute the edges and prick the top. Bake in a 400-degree oven for 1 hour 15 minutes or until pastry is browned. Serves 4-6.

Dutch Apple Pie

Crust
- 1 cup flour
- 1/2 cup shortening
- 1 egg

Beat together above ingredients and pat out with hands into pie plate. Don't roll. Fill crust with thin sliced apples, sprinkle with 1 cup sugar, dust on cinnamon to suit taste. Beat one egg, 4 tablespoons cream, 1 teaspoon vanilla together and pour over apples. Bake in 400-degree oven for 10 minutes. Reduce heat to 300 degrees and finish baking about 1 hour all together.

Serve with vanilla ice cream or whipped cream.

American Vanilla Ice Cream

Makes about 1 1/2 quarts
- 1 envelope unflavored gelatin
- 1 cup cold water
- 1 14-oz. can sweetened condensed milk
- 2 cups light cream
- 1 Tbls vanilla extract

In small sauce pan soften gelatin in 1/4 cup water, heat and stir until dissolved. Stir in remaining water. Proceed according to desired method.

Electric or Hand-Turned Ice Cream Freezer
Combine softened gelatin and remaining ingredients in ice cream freezer container. Follow manufacturers instructions.

Refrigerator-Freezer Method
In large bowl combine softened gelatin and blend remaining ingredients. Blend Well. Turn into 13 x 9-inch baking pan; freeze to a firm mush (about 1 hr). Break into pieces and turn into chilled, large mixer bowl; beat until smooth. Return to the pan. Cover with foil and freeze until firm.

Variations
Georgia Peach — Reduce vanilla to 2 teaspoons and add one tsp almond extract; add 1 cup mashed fresh peaches or 1 16-oz. can peaches, drained and finely chopped, to vanilla ice cream.

Fresh and Fancy Strawberry — Add 2 cups well mashed fresh strawberries to vanilla ice cream.

Flapper Pie

Graham Cracker Crust
- 7 wafers
- 1/2 cup brown sugar
- 1/4 cup melted butter

Mix together and save 1/4 cup for topping. Press into pie pan.

- 2 cups heated milk
- 2 eggs
- 1/2 cup sugar
- 2 Tbls flour

Mix egg mixture and milk together. Heat and stir until mixture coats the back of a spoon (about 5 minutes). Add vanilla and take off stove. Cool in frig before putting in pie shell.

Meringue
- 3 egg whites
- 4 Tbls powdered sugar

Beat egg whites until stiff. Add powdered sugar. Put on top of pie and sprinkle with 1/4 cup of crumb mixture.

❦ Mary Emily Murray Smith
    Emily, Dannette, and Claire's paternal grandmother

Flower Garden Cake

- 6 egg yolks
- 6 egg whites
- 1 1/2 cups sugar
- 1 1/2 envelopes unflavored gelatin
- 1/4 cup cold water
- 3/4 cup lemon juice
- grated rind of 2 lemons
- grated rind and juice of one orange
- 1 large angel food cake

Beat eggs yolks and add 3/4 cup sugar, juices and rind. Cook in double boiler until it begins to thicken. Remove from stove, add gelatin, which has been soaking in 1/4 cup cold water. Stir until dissolved. Beat egg whites until stiff, add remainder of sugar (3/4 cup) to the whites. Fold into the custard. Break cake into small pieces. Stir cake into custard. Pour all into well greased torte pan. Set in refrigerator for several hours to set. Remove from pan and ice with sweetened whipped cream.

Place on a tray decorated with fresh flowers.
The same idea may be used with a rum or chocolate custard.

Rum Custard
- 1 1/4 cups sugar
- 3 eggs
- 3 cups milk
- 1/8 tsp salt

Cook to a custard. Add 2 1/2 packages gelatin that has been softened in 3/4 cup cold water. Add 1 cup rum.

Chocolate Custard
Same as rum except substitute 2 squares melted unsweetened chocolate for the rum and add 1 teaspoon vanilla.

❦ Christine Griffin
      Marci's sister-in-law

Dan and Sugah

Dan is my brother. I'm six years older than he is. In fact my mother was in the hospital having just birthed him on my first day of school. My aunt, LaRue, was in the third grade so on my first day of school my grandmother let me wear one of LaRue's dresses (you know it was cute — at least 6 inches too long and hanging off the shoulders — but I thought I looked good) and off to school we walked because it was only two blocks.

Being that much older than Dan, I do have some clear memories of early family years. And they were wonderful. We lived in the panhandle of Florida and had a real Huck Finn-type existence. We lived two blocks from St. Joe Bay, and could walk there and collect shells and pieces of pottery shards which we were told were left over from the Great Tidal Wave and the Yellow Fever epidemic. We lived on Monument Ave. near town. The other way was Monument Park which had a big granite monument dedicated to the memory of those early brave ones who had settled St. Joseph and died there.

But back to Dan. He had asthma as a baby and toddler. I'm sure that corn cob pipe he smoked didn't help his breathing difficulties much, but what he would do was find any kind of fluff, feather or cotton and tuck it into his pointer finger, then suck his thumb while he tickled his nose with the soft stuff he had in his finger. He was a contented kid when he was doing that. But because of the asthma all the feather pillows in the house had to go. Then all the teddy bears and stuffed animals. Still he continued to have asthma attacks. One time we were visiting the local zoo. We were watching the antics of the monkeys when somebody missed Dan. We found him. He was caught in the fence around the duck pond. He had spied a molted feather near the fence and had reached in to get it. He would not turn it loose to get his hand back through the fence.

We had a beautiful black and white cat named Sugah. Sugah was a big male cat with the beautiful white chest and white boots. He and Dan were inseparable. Even after Dan put him in the clothes dryer, they still were never apart. Nobody inspected Sugah, so things had gotten really out of hand before any one noticed that Sugah had no chest hair left. He was picked clean. Not a white hair left. Dan would reach over, pull a curled finger of hair out and suck his thumb and tickle his nose. The old cat just lay there purring.

We have a name for that now. It's called co-dependency. Although the relationship is damaging to both partners — one has asthma the other has no protective hair — they continue their destructive relationship regardless of the emotional and physical costs to each partner. I don't know when, but at some point Dan quit sucking his thumb and Sugah grew back his beautiful chest of white hair. It's usually not that easy or uneventful. The answer to the co-dependency issue is to put your faith, trust and life in God's hands, not into another human being's.

Galatians 1:10 — *Am I seeking the favor of men, or of God?*

Hard Sauce

- 1 cup confectioner's sugar
- 2-5 Tbls butter
- 1/8 tsp salt
- 1 tsp vanilla, coffee, rum, whisky, brandy, lemon or orange juice
- 1 egg or 1/4 cup cream

Cream the softened butter in a small bowl at high speed. Add the sugar gradually. Add the flavoring. Beat the sauce until it is creamy, about 5 minutes. Scrape the sides of the bowl once or twice while beating. Chill the sauce.

French Vanilla Pound Cake

- 1 box French vanilla Jello instant pudding mix
- 1 package Duncan Hines Deluxe yellow cake mix
- 1 cup unsweetened apple juice
- 3/4 cup Wesson oil
- 4 eggs
- 1 Tbls vanilla

Mix together all the dry ingredients. Add alternately, one egg, oil, apple juice until all is well mixed. Beat well with electric beater until smooth. Grease and flour a 10-inch tube pan. Pour mixture in. Bake at 350 degrees for about 40 minutes. Do not overcook.

🌼 Ina Mae Creech Dillon

Aunt Maizy says: "Wrap the cake with Glad Wrap then with aluminum foil so cake will be air tight. Put in refrigerator for a day and night before opening and start eating. Always wrap cake after each time of eating, will last a very long time."

Frozen Chocolate Brownie Pie

- 1/4 cup margarine
- 2/3 cup firmly packed brown sugar
- 1/2 cup egg substitute
- 1/4 cup buttermilk
- 1/4 cup all purpose flour
- 1/3 cup cocoa
- 1/4 tsp salt
- 1 tsp vanilla
- vegetable cooking spray
- 1/2 gal vanilla nonfat frozen yogurt, softened
- 1 qt chocolate nonfat frozen yogurt, softened
- 3/4 cup chocolate syrup

Melt margarine in a large sauce over medium high heat, add brown sugar, stirring with a wire whisk. Remove from heat; cool slightly. Add egg substitute and buttermilk, stirring well. Combine flour, cocoa, and salt. Add to buttermilk mixture, stirring until blended. Stir in vanilla. Pour into a 9-inch spring form pan lightly coated with cooking spray. Bake at 350 degrees for 15 minutes. Cool completely in pan on a wire rack.

Spread half of vanilla yogurt over brownie; cover and freeze until firm. Spread chocolate yogurt over vanilla yogurt; cover and freeze until firm. Top with remaining vanilla yogurt. Cover and freeze at least 8 hours.

Remove sides of pan. Serve each wedge with 1 tablespoon syrup. Garnish with strawberries and/or chocolate curls.

Fruit Cocktail Cake

- 2 eggs-well beaten
- 2 cups flour
- 1 1/2 cups sugar
- 2 tsp soda
- 1 can #303 fruit cocktail

Note: no shortening in cake dough.
Sift flour, sugar and soda together over well beaten eggs. Add Fruit Cocktail and juice and beat lightly with spoon. Not mix master. Pour in well greased, waxed paper-lined pans. Bake about 25 to 30 minutes at 325 degrees.

Icing
- 1 1/2 sticks Butter or margarine
- 1 small can Evaporated Milk or slightly less
- 1 1/2 cups sugar
- 1 cup chopped nuts
- 1 cup coconut, firmly packed

Mix ingredients in order listed, in boiler and boil about 8 or 10 min. Stir so it won't burn. Spread on layers, sides and top while either hot or cold.

Lina: "I prefer both to be slightly warm, I put mine in the freezer a short time so the icing will stick, and then wrap in aluminum foil. It does nicely frozen and is never hard to slice."

❦ Lina Creech Bouton

Marci Griffin says: "Aunt Nina brought this cake to a family reunion at Charles' river home about 35 years ago. It was so delicious I made her send me the recipe. And I have baked it many times. It is rich but so yummy!"

Grannie Horn's Lane Cake

Makes 2 cakes, use half for average cake.

- 3 1/2 cups flour
- 2 cups sugar
- 8 egg whites
- 1 cup milk
- 1 cup butter
- 2 tsp baking powder
- 1 tsp vanilla

Cream butter, sugar, add flour gradually. Beat egg whites separately until stiff not dry; add to mixture. Pour into three cake pans. Bake (I'm guessing 350 degrees until the cake bounces back when you touch the middle), about 25 minutes.

Filling (Icing)
- 8 egg yolks
- 2 cups sugar
- 1 cup milk
- 1 can or package frozen grated coconut (unsweetened if you can get it)
- 1 cup pecans, well-chopped
- 1 cup raisins minced
- wine glass of brandy or wine
     Grannie says, "I use whiskey!"

 Combine all ingredients in top of double boiler (except whiskey). Cook until very thick. Add whiskey just before taking from stove. Cool both cake and Icing before icing. Ice between cakes and top and sides. Hold layers in place with tooth picks if needed.

This is an Alabama cake. Only people in Alabama, south Georgia and south Mississippi have ever heard of it.

Granny Horn was Daddy Rue's Mother. My great-grandmother.

Grandmother's Quick Kuchen

- 1 cup sugar
- 1/2 cup butter or margarine
- 2 cups flour
- 1/2 cup milk
- 3 eggs, well beaten
- 1 tsp vanilla (I use half vanilla and half almond flavoring)
- 2 tsp baking powder

Cream sugar and butter. Use an electric beater if you have one. Add to this the measured flour, measured before sifting, and sifted twice afterward, the last time with the baking powder, alternating flour with the milk, and last of all, fold in the well beaten eggs and vanilla. Pour into a long, greased rectangular biscuit pan with 1 1/2-inch sides.
Sprinkle with the following mixture:
- 1 Tbls cinnamon
- 1/4 cup sugar
- 1/4 cup chopped pecans or almonds

Bake in 375-degree oven 15-20 minutes. Cut into 1 1/2-inch squares when cool. Half the recipe will fill a 9 x 9 pan. When the recipe is halved, use 1 whole egg and an extra white or yolk.

Variation — Praline Frosting
1 cup brown sugar
2 Tbls flour
1/2 cup melted butter
2 Tbls water
1/2 tsp vanilla
1 cup coarsely chopped pecans, or any preferred nuts.

Mix the brown sugar with the flour, butter, water, vanilla, and nuts. Spread evenly over the cake as it is taken from the oven. Run back under flame of broiler as it is taken from the oven. Let it remain until icing bubbles and browns to form a glazed surface. When cool, cut into squares.

This is Bertha Kahn's grandmother's recipe. She was a friend of my mother's in the real estate business in Montgomery and took an interest in me as a young bride.

Ginger Bread

This recipe is 140 years old.

- 1 cup sugar
- 1/2 cup shortening
- 2 eggs
- 1 cup molasses
- 1 cup buttermilk
- 3 cups flour
- 1 tsp cloves
- 2 tsp soda
- 2 tsp ginger
- 1 tsp nutmeg
- 1/3 cup chocolate syrup

Cream sugar and shortening, add eggs, buttermilk and molasses and chocolate syrup. Mix dry ingredients and add to first mixture. Beat well. Bake in 325-degree oven 40-45 minutes. Using Pam, spray a 13 x 9 x 2-inch pan or glass dish.

❦ Lu Gibson

Lemon Sauce
- 3/4 cup confectioner's sugar
- 3 Tbls butter
- 2 eggs
- 1/2 cup boiling water
- 1 tsp grated lemon rind
- 3 Tbls lemon juice or 2 Tbls brandy

Beat butter until soft, and add the sifted confectioner's sugar until they are creamy. Beat in the 2 eggs and then slowly stir in the hot water. Cook and stir in a double boiler or over a very low flame until it thickens. Remove it from the heat. Stir in the lemon rind, the juice or the brandy.

Ginger Bread

- 1/3 cup shortening
- 1 cup sugar
- 2 eggs
- 1/2 cup molasses
- 1 cup sour cream
- 2 cups sifted flour
- 1 tsp soda
- 1/2 tsp salt
- 1 tsp grated lemon or orange rind
- 1 1/2 tsp ground ginger
- 1/4 tsp ground cloves

Cream shortening and sugar; add eggs, one at a time, beating well after each addition. Stir in molasses and sour cream. Blend sifted dry ingredients into creamed mixture; beat 2 minutes at medium speed. Bake in greased 13 x 9 x 2-inch pan at 350 degrees for 35 minutes, or until cake tests done.

Topping
- 1/4 cup brown sugar
- 1 tsp cinnamon
- 2 Tbls flour
- 2 Tbls butter

Work with hands until crumbly then add 1/2 cup chopped nut meats. Spread on 10 minutes before baking is done.

Lemon Sauce
- 3/4 cup confectioner's sugar
- 3 Tbls butter
- 2 eggs
- 1/2 cup boiling water
- 1 tsp grated lemon rind
- 3 Tbls lemon juice or 2 Tbls brandy

Beat butter until soft, and add the sifted confectioner's sugar until they are creamy. Beat in the 2 eggs and then slowly stir in the hot water. Cook and stir in a double boiler or over a very low flame until it thickens. Remove from heat. Stir in the lemon rind, the juice or the brandy.

Driving Miss Maureene

The early summer before I entered the seminary I was trying to raise money at every turn, so when Maureene asked me to drive her all over Montgomery one day I jumped at it. Maureene was leaving for Paraguay the following day to see her daughter, son-in-law and grandson and the week before had stepped off a curb and severely sprained her ankle. She was bandaged and on crutches at this point and unable to drive. She offered to pay me $100 for the day — not to be sneezed at in my book.

We started out that morning by going to her office, across the street to First National Bank, then downtown to Union Bank and then back to First National Bank from where we had just been 30 minutes before. I noticed I was mentally trying to organize us and I was gripping the steering wheel and just generally getting my panties in a wad over our scattered approach to Maureene's errands.

We did this same stuff everyday and I always immensely enjoyed our time together. What was so different about today? Then I got it.

Maureene paid me to drive her. That meant I was working for her. That meant that I had to take my job seriously. That meant no fun. Work is serious business. The message I had gotten all my life is how you have to give your work your all. At the end of the day you were exhausted because you had worked so hard.

If I went to the seminary and graduated as a minister and went out to serve God in my work, I would be burned out in a year because I would work so hard and take it so seriously that all the fun would go out of it. That attitude had to change. The reason I had chosen to go to the seminary was because I loved all the reading, I loved counseling, I loved giving the lessons (preaching), I loved sharing my experience, strength and hope. I loved it all.

I found when I went out into the field that I could do all aspects of my job and enjoy it and have fun with it and give humorous sermons even when they had serious points to them. I could have fun and be paid for it.

Reverend Edwene Gaines said it first that I know of: "Being a success is doing what you love to do, and doing it so well that people will pay you well for doing it."

Amen!

Honey Date Bars

- 1 cup honey
- 3 eggs, well beaten
- 1 tsp vanilla
- 1 1/3 cups sifted flour
- 1 tsp baking powder
- 1/2 tsp salt
- 2 7-1/4-oz. packages pitted dates, cut up
- 1 cup chopped nuts
- fine granulated sugar

Mix honey, eggs and vanilla; beat well. Add sifted dry ingredients, dates and nuts. Spread in greased 13 x 9 x 2-inch pan. Bake in moderate oven at 350 degrees for about 45 minutes. Cool in pan. Cut in 1 x 3-inch bars and roll in sugar.

Ozark Pudding

- 4 eggs
- 2 1/2 cups sugar
- 1/2 cup + 2 Tbls flour
- 1 3/4 tsp baking powder
- 1/2 tsp salt
- 2 cups finely chopped apples
- 2 cups chopped nuts
- 2 Tsp vanilla

Mix sugar with beaten eggs and vanilla. Mix dry ingredients, add nuts and apples. Grease 13 x 9 x 2-inch pan. Pour mixture into pan and bake in 300-degree oven for 40 minutes or until lightly brown. Serve with Cool Whip.

❦ Lu Gibson

Hummingbird Cake

- 3 cups all-purpose flour
- 2 cups sugar
- 1 tsp baking soda
- 1 tsp salt
- 1 tsp ground cinnamon
- 3 eggs, beaten
- 1 cup vegetable oil
- 1 1/2 tsp vanilla
- 1 8-oz. can crushed pineapple, undrained
- 1 cup chopped pecans
- 2 cups chopped bananas
- cream cheese frosting (see below)
- 1/2 cup chopped pecans

Combine first five ingredients in a large mixing bowl; add eggs and oil, stirring until dry ingredients are moistened. Do not beat. Stir in vanilla, pineapple,1 cup pecans and bananas.

Spoon batter into three greased and floured 9-inch round cake pans. Bake at 350 degrees for 25-30 minutes or until a wooden pick inserted in center comes out clean. Cool in pans 10 minutes. Remove from pans and cool completely.

Spread frosting between layers and on top and sides of cake; then sprinkle 1/2 cup chopped pecans on top. Makes one 3-layer cake.

Cream Cheese Frosting
- 1 8-oz. package cream cheese, softened
- 1/2 cup butter or margarine, softened
- 1 16-oz. pkg powdered sugar sifted
- 1 tsp vanilla

Combine cream cheese and butter, beating until smooth. Add powdered sugar and vanilla; beat until light and fluffy. Makes enough frosting for one 3-layer cake.

Lane cake

- 1 cup butter
- 2 cups sugar
- 3 1/2 cups cake flour
- 2 tsps baking powder
- 1 cup milk
- pinch salt
- 1 tsp vanilla
- 7 egg whites (beaten stiff but not dry)

Have ingredients at room temperature. Cream butter and sugar together until fluffy. Add sifted dry ingredients alternately with milk. Add vanilla, fold in beaten egg whites. Pour into two greased and floured pans and bake at 350 degrees for 25 to 30 minutes. Put layers together with filling.

Lane Cake Filling
- 7 egg yolks, beaten
- 1 cup sugar
- 1/2 cup butter
- pinch salt
- 1 cup chopped pecans
- 1 cup chopped raisins
- 1 cup grated coconut
- 1/2 cup wine

Combine egg yolks, sugar and butter in top of double boiler and cook over hot water until thick, stirring constantly. Let cool some and then add salt, coconut, nuts and raisins. Stir in wine. Spread generously between layers and on top and sides of cake. Sprinkle more grated coconut on top of cake.

Lemon Cheese Cake

- 1 cup butter
- 2 cups sugar
- 1 cup milk (1/2 cup milk, 1/2 cup water)
- 3 cups flour
- 8 egg whites (not beaten)
- 3 Tbls baking powder
- 1 tsp vanilla
- pinch salt

Cream butter and sugar, add milk and egg whites alternately and salt and vanilla. Bake in oven at 350 degrees for about 20 minutes. Makes 4 layers.

Lemon Cheese Filling
- 8 egg yolks
- 1 cup sugar
- 1 can crushed pineapple (small can). Drain juice off.
- 3 Tbls butter
- 2 lemons, grated and juice

Cook ingredients until thick, add pineapple and cook about 5 minutes more.

7-Minute Icing
- 2 egg whites, unbeaten
- 1 1/2 cups sugar
- 5 Tbls cold water
- 1/8 tsp salt
- 1 1/2 Tbls light corn syrup

Place over boiling water in a double boiler, beat on #1 speed until blended, then cook, beating constantly on #9 speed until mixture will stand in peaks, add 1 tsp vanilla, continue beating until spreading consistency, about 5 minutes.

❤ Billie Creech Horne

Lemon Sauce

- 3/4 cup confectioner's sugar
- 3 Tbls butter
- 2 eggs
- 1/2 cup boiling water
- 1 tsp grated lemon rind
- 3 Tbls lemon juice or 2 Tbls brandy

Beat butter until soft, and add the sifted confectioner's sugar until they are creamy. Beat in the 2 eggs and then slowly stir in the hot water. Cook and stir in a double boiler or over a very low flame until it thickens. Remove it from the heat. Stir in the lemon rind, the juice or the brandy.

Lina's Apricot-Coconut Balls

- 1 8-oz. pkg dried apricots, grind
- 2 cups shredded coconut
- 2/3 cup sweetened condensed milk

Mix together in order listed. Shape into small balls. Let stand out in the air about one hour. Then re-roll (this seems to remove moisture, or pack them more firmly). Before serving, sprinkle very lightly with powdered sugar.

❦ Lina (or Nina) Bouton, Grandmother Horn's sister.
> *The Creech siblings were Leila, Nina, Frances, Ina Mae (Maizy) Billie, Kenneth, Gus, Charles Creech.*

Lemon Tea Bread

- 3/4 cup milk
- 1 Tbls chopped fresh lemon juice
- 1 Tbls chopped lemon thyme or 1 tsp dried thyme
- 1/2 cup butter or margarine
- 1 cup sugar
- 2 large eggs
- 2 cups all purpose flour
- 1 1/2 tsp baking powder
- 1/4 tsp salt
- 1 Tbls grated lemon rind
- lemon glaze (see below)

Combine first three ingredients in a saucepan; bring to a boil. remove from heat, cover and let stand 5 minutes. Cool. Beat butter at medium speed with an electric mixer until creamy; gradually add sugar, beating well. Add eggs, one at a time, beating after each addition. Combine next three ingredients, add to butter mixture alternately with milk mixture, beginning and ending with flour mixture. Mix after each addition. Stir in lemon rind. Pour batter into a greased and floured 9 x 5 x 3-inch loaf pan. Bake at 325 degrees for 50 minutes or until a wooden pick inserted in center comes out clean. Cool in pan on a wire rack 10 minutes. Remove from pan, and cool completely. Pour glaze over bread. Makes 1 loaf.

Lemon Glaze
- 1 cup sifted powdered sugar
- 2 Tbls lemon juice

Combine and stir until smooth. Makes 1/3 cup.

Mama's Fudge

- 4 1/2 cups sugar
- 1 large can evaporated milk

Boil together 12 minutes, stirring constantly.

- 3 packages chocolate morsels
- 2 sticks butter
- 1 jar marshmallow cream

Put in a bowl, slowly pour the hot fudge mixture over the sugar and milk stirring all the while. Stir real good. Add 2-3 cups chopped pecans, beat until smooth. Pour in buttered pan and let cool. Cut in squares.

❦ Annette Brooks

I will never forget walking in while Mama was on her reducing machine. You laid on this contraption and the middle part, which was beneath your waist, stomach and thighs, rocked back and forth — I guess to massage the fat off you. She had a small plate of this fudge on her stomach. She rocked and ate fudge. She just died laughing when I came in.

No Fail Pie Crust

- 3 cups flour, sift with salt
- 1 tsp salt
- 5 Tbls water
- 1 1/4 cup shortening
- 1 egg well beaten
- 1 Tbls vinegar

Cut flour into shortening. Combine water, egg, vinegar, and pour into flour and shortening. Blend until all moistened. Roll out on floured board

Makes 4 single crusts. (You can freeze these crusts.)

❦ Pat Griggs

Meringue

- 3 egg whites
- 1/4 cup sugar

Beat egg whites until stiff peaks form, add sugar slowly while beating constantly.

Mamas' Hints
To make a good meringue for pie, add a pinch of cream of tarter while beating egg whites stiff. Preheat oven. Cut it off and put pie in oven for meringue to brown.

Mrs Hagedorn's Pecan Torte

- 8 eggs, separated
- 1 1/2 cups sugar
- 1/2 cup cracker meal or matzo meal
- 1 tsp baking powder
- pinch salt
- juice 1/2 lemon
- 1 tsp vanilla
- 1/2 lb ground pecans

Beat eggs yolks with sugar. Add salt. Mix meal with baking powder. Add to egg yolks. Then add the ground pecans, lemon juice and vanilla. Fold in the stiffly beaten whites. Pour into well greased and floured 9 x 13 x 2 pan. Bake at 325 degrees for about one hour. Ice when cold.

Icing

Melt 1/4 stick butter or margarine. Add 2 cups sifted powdered sugar, two or three tablespoons sifted cocoa, one teaspoon vanilla and enough cold coffee to moisten to spreading consistency.

Mrs. Hagedorn is the mother of two spinster sisters who were physical education teachers at Lanier High School (circa 1940s and 1950s) in Montgomery. Miss Nell (I don't know the other's name) and her sister were in their 50s at that time. You always knew Mrs. Hagedorn and later the sisters: they drove about a 1950 or '51 Plymouth and all you could see from the rear were two hands on the steering wheel. It was only when you passed could you see the little person who was driving.

Miss Bertha Kahn gave me this recipe. Her family was a partner in the Schloss and Kahn Canning Co., makers of Sunday Dinner products.

Exploring with Effie

My friend Florence and I were probably the two most innocent girls in the senior class. Our motives and interests were on a higher plane but speaking for me I could sure get into some major trouble with my high ideals.

The summer of 1957, I was working in the Revenue Dept. for the State of Alabama as a temporary employee. Florence and I decided we would go exploring, so I skipped work and we gathered up the contents for a sack lunch and went up to some isolated place at one of the lakes near Montgomery and had a picnic and communed with nature. Unbeknownst to us, my younger brother, Dan, who was a page at the legislature, had come by my office at the Revenue Dept. to say hello and discovered that I had not come to work that morning. Big Mouth couldn't wait to call home with that little news flash.

After we ate, we headed on back to Montgomery; Florence went home and I went out to Mt. Meigs and parked under a huge oak tree and waited for my boy friend to pass as he was headed home from Auburn University for the weekend. I waited several hours and was getting really put out with him for being so late when that black and white lowered '54 Ford with glass-packed Trutones flew by. I had a little '48 Chevrolet coupe with a leaky radiator without a prayer of catching up with him, so I headed for Pop's Coke Stand and hoped he would come by. Well, he did. He pulled up beside my car, rolled down his car window and said, "Get your butt home this minute!" My lower lip started quivering and I said, "Don't talk to me like that," and with his face as red as a beet he fairly yelled at me: "I've been held at the police station in Auburn under hot lights for three hours being grilled about where you are. Your folks think we have eloped. The state troopers are out in Alabama, Georgia and Mississippi looking for you!"

I went home to find the family wringing their hands over me. I'm sure my nonchalance about the whole situation made Mama and Daddy want to beat me half to death. To really add insult to injury, out-of-town company had come for the weekend and their response was, "We didn't know you were having trouble with Patti."

That little escapade of mine and Florence's caused me to get sent 800 miles from home to school to get me as far away as possible from Mr. '54 Ford. It worked.

A wonderful scripture reads: *Vengeance is mine saith the Lord* — **Romans 12:19.** I finished growing up and had three daughters. The apple doesn't fall far from the tree.

Mud Pie

- 1 cup sugar
- 1/2 cup shortening
- 2 eggs
- 1/8 tsp salt
- 3/4 cup flour
- 1/4 cup cocoa
- 1 1/2 tsp vanilla
- 1/4 cup chopped nuts
- 1/2 package small marshmallows

Cream sugar and shortening together, add eggs while still beating. Sift cocoa, flour and salt and add. Pour into an 8 x 8 pan. Add vanilla, nuts, bake at 300 degrees for 30 minutes. Top with marshmallows and continue baking until they are browned. Cool completely.

Icing
- 1/4 cup margarine or butter
- 1/2 box powdered sugar
- 1/4 cup cocoa
- 1/4 cup evaporated milk
- 1/2 tsp vanilla
- 1/4 cup chopped nuts.

Melt margarine, add sifted sugar and cocoa to melted margarine, cool until slightly soft, then ice the pie.

Mud Pie (Frozen)

- chocolate crumb pie shell (Oreo cookies and butter)
- 1 pint coffee ice cream
- hot chocolate sauce

Fill shell with ice cream and freeze. Remove form freezer about ten minutes before serving. Serve with hot sauce.

❤ Marci Griffin

Pat Grigg's Pecan Pie

- 1/4 cup butter
- 1/2 cup sugar
- 1 cup dark Karo
- 1/4 tsp salt
- 3 eggs
- 1 cup pecans

Cream butter and sugar. Pour in salt and syrup. Beat each egg into mixture one at the time. Add pecans, pour into pie crust unbaked and pricked. Bake at 350 degrees for 55 minutes.

No Fail Pie Crust
- 3 cups flour, sift with salt
- 1 tsp salt
- 5 Tbls water
- 1 1/4 cup shortening
- 1 egg well beaten
- 1 Tbls vinegar

Cut flour into shortening. Combine water, egg, vinegar, and pour into flour and shortening. Blend until all moistened. Roll out on floured board.

Makes 4 single crusts. (You can freeze these crusts.)

Peanut Angel Squares

- 1 12-oz. loaf angel food cake, cut in 2-inch squares
- 1 cup butter
- 1 lb confectioner's sugar
- 1 tsp vanilla
- 1/3 to 1/2 cup cream
- 1/4 tsp salt
- 1/4 cup cocoa
- 1 tsp instant coffee
- 2 cups crushed roasted peanuts

Cream butter,add vanilla, salt, cocoa, coffee, add about half of sugar; mix. Add about 4 tsps cream; mix. Add rest of sugar; mix. Then add enough cream to spread mixture. Frost 3 sides of cake square and roll in crushed peanuts. Freeze. Thaw when ready to use.

"This can be made days ahead. Sure is good, too." Billie Creech Horne.

Pound Cake

- 1/2 lb butter
- 6 eggs
- 2 1/2 cups sugar
- 3 cups flour
- 1/2 tsp baking soda
- 1 carton or 1 cup (8 oz) sour cream
- 2 tsps vanilla (or almond) flavoring

Cream butter and sugar well. Put in eggs one at the time, beat each egg one minute. Add flour, cup at the time, beating well. Then add sour cream with soda and flavoring. Stir batter just long enough to mix well. Bake in bundt (tube) pan in preheated oven 350 degrees for 1 hour and 10 minutes. If center seems a little soft, turn off the oven and let stand in oven for 10 minutes.

❦ Billie Creech Horne

Pecan Fudge Pie

You need a large (deep dish) frozen pie shell.

- 1 12-oz. package semisweet chocolate pieces
- 4 eggs
- 1/2 tsp salt
- 2 tsp vanilla
- 1 cup light corn syrup
- 2 Tbls butter or margarine, melted
- 1 1/2 cups halved or coarsely chopped pecans
- 1 unbaked 9-inch pie shell

Preheat oven to 350 degrees. In small saucepan over low heat, melt chocolate pieces, stirring occasionally. In a medium bowl, beat together next 5 ingredients. Slowly add melted chocolate, stirring rapidly with a wire whisk or spoon. Fold in pecans, pour into pie shell. Bake at 350 degrees for about 50 to 60 minutes or until center is set. Cool. Makes 10-12 servings

Without the pecans, this is fudge pie.

Pot de Cream

- 1 cup semi-sweet chocolate chips
- 1 1/4 cups light cream, scalded
- 2 egg yolks
- 3 Tbls brandy

Put all ingredients in blender-cover and process on medium until smooth. Pour into cups filling 2/3 full. Cover and chill at least 3 hours. Top with whipped cream.

Prune Whip

- 1 lb dried prunes, stewed
- 5 egg whites
- 1/8 tsp salt
- 1/4 tsp cream of tartar or 1/4 tsp lemon juice added to the prunes
- 1/2 cup sugar
- 1 tsp grated lemon rind

Cover dried prunes with water and 1/2 cup sugar and simmer until soft. Add a little more water if needed to keep the prunes simmering in water. When done, remove the pits and beat up the prunes in a blender. Whip until foamy, egg whites and 1/8 tsp salt. Add the cream of tartar and beat egg whites until stiff. Fold egg whites and prunes together. Place souffle in a 9-inch baking dish. Set in a pan of hot water. Bake it in a slow oven at 275 degrees for about 1 hour until it is firm. Serve hot or cold.

May be served with lemon custard sauce or whipped cream on top.

Lemon Custard Sauce
- 2 eggs, beat until light
- 1/2 cup sugar, beat in gradually
- 1/2 tsp grated lemon rind
- 1/8 tsp salt

Place bowl over hot water. Beat the custard until the sugar is dissolved and the sauce is warm. Add 1/2 cup lukewarm milk. Beat 1 minute longer and add 1 Tbls lemon juice.

Faith and Trust

Have you ever been told that you don't have enough faith? Do you know the difference between faith and trust?

In Hebrews 11:1, Paul says, "Now faith is the assurance of things hoped for, the conviction of things not seen."

Charles Fillmore, co-founder of Unity says faith is "the perceiving power of the mind linked with the ability to shape substance."

Faith is that inborn feeling we have. It's linked with hope. Paul tells us that it is the knowing that what we hope for will materialize even though we can't see it now. It's one of the powers innate in humankind. Charles Fillmore tells us that it is the ability of our imagination to see things and to call them forth into the visible.

Trust, on the other hand, is a choice we make. For those of us who were born in dysfunctional families, and most of us were, love was conditional — if you behave in a certain way then you earn my love. Love could be easily withdrawn by a parent in disapproval or so it seemed to the totally dependent, vulnerable child. This helped destroy trust. As adults we work to rebuild and reestablish this thing called trust, but not necessarily on other people. Humans must prove their trustworthiness by their behavior.

As adults we learn to rely on God or our Higher power. We have faith that God is with us and loves us unconditionally. This is a feeling and a knowing in our hearts. To activate trust, we must choose to activate it.

The dictionary defines trust as: 1) Firm reliance on the integrity, ability, or character of a person or thing. 2) Custody; care.

We do this by choosing to trust in God. It is a conscious choice. As we daily practice this choice we find that God has an excellent track record for being dependable and loving. As time goes on we demonstrate this over and over and realize that this is indeed a loving universe, run by a trustworthy Power.

This loving Universe that becomes part of our experience in life is a direct result of using the faith we're born with, and coupling it with our deliberate choice to trust in this Higher Power or God. Yes, we are the beloved children of God.

Raspberry-Cherry Cobbler

- 1 16-oz. package frozen unsweetened raspberries, thawed
- 1 16-oz. package frozen no sugar added pitted dark sweet cherries, thawed
- 1 cup sugar
- 1/4 cup all purpose flour
- 1 Tbls lemon juice
- 1/8 tsp ground cinnamon
- vegetable cooking spray
- 2 cups flour
- 1 Tbls baking powder
- 1 tsp baking soda
- 1 tsp salt
- 2 Tbls sugar
- 1/4 cup reduced calorie margarine
- 3/4 cup plain nonfat yogurt
- 1/4 cup evaporated skimmed milk

Combine first six ingredients; spoon into an 11 x 7 x 1 1/2-inch baking dish coated with cooking spray. Combine 2 cups flour and next four ingredients in a large bowl; cut in margarine with a pastry blender until mixture is crumbly. Add yogurt and milk, stirring with a fork until dry ingredients are moistened. Turn dough out onto a lightly floured surface, and knead about 10 times. Roll dough to 1/2-inch thickness; cut 12 rounds using 1/2-inch cutter. Cut 6 diamonds from remaining dough.

Arrange biscuit rounds and diamond shapes on top of fruit mixture. Bake at 425 degrees for 20-25 minutes or until bubbly and biscuits are golden brown, remove from oven; lightly coat each biscuit with cooking spray. Makes 12 servings

Scotch Shortbreads

Makes 1 dozen.

- 2-1/2 cups sifted flour
- 1/4 tsp salt
- 1/2 cup confectioner's sugar
- 1 cup butter
- blanched almonds
- candied cherries
- angelica or citron

Sift dry ingredients into bowl. Break butter in small pieces, and work in dry ingredients with hands until mixture is smooth and blended. Halve dough, and roll each half to form a 6-inch round, 1/2 inch thick. Put on brown paper on cookie sheet. With tines of fork, outline 6 wedges in each round. Prick wedges with fork. Decorate with almonds, bit of cherry and andelica or citron. Bake in slow oven, 275 degrees for about 45 minutes. Remove to wire racks and cool. Break apart.

Shoofly Pie

- 1 1/2 cups all purpose flour
- 1 1/4 cups firmly packed dark brown sugar, divided
- 1/2 tsp salt
- 1/2 cup butter
- 1/2 cup boiling water
- 1 tsp soda
- 1/2 cup molasses
- 1 unbaked 9-inch pie shell

Combine flour, 1 cup sugar and salt. Add butter, and cut in with a pastry blender until mixture is crumble; reserve 1/2 cup crumbs to sprinkle on top of pie. Combine water and soda; add molasses and remaining sugar. Stir molasses mixture into crumbs and pour into pie shell. Sprinkle reserved crumbs over top. Bake at 350 degrees for 35-40 minutes. Cool before serving.

Vanilla Wafer Cake

- 1 cup butter
- 1 12-oz. box vanilla wafers
- 2 cups sugar
- 1 4-oz. can coconut
- 6 whole eggs
- 1 cup chopped pecans

Cream butter and sugar, add eggs-add crushed wafers, the coconut and pecans. Stir well. Bake at 300 degrees for about 45 minutes. (Every oven differs; you might need an hour. It will be golden brown on top and firm to the touch.) Serve from pan. (Freezes great.)

Cream Cheese Frosting
- 1 8-oz. pkg cream cheese
- 1 stick butter softened
- 1 box powdered sugar
- 1 tsp vanilla
- 1/2 cup chopped nuts

Spread when the cake is cool. Bake ahead and freeze. Remove from freezer at least 2 hours before serving. Cut and serve from the pan.

❦ Cornelia Baum

This is the most fabulous cake in the world — extra easy — and very rich.

Sour Cream Pound Cake

- 1/2 lb butter
- 6 eggs
- 3 cups sugar
- 3 cups flour
- 1/2 pint sour cream
- 2 tsp vanilla
- 1/4 tsp soda
- 1/2 tsp salt

Separate eggs; beat whites until stiff, add 1/2 cup sugar, and beat yolk. Set aside. Cream butter and 2 1/2 cups sugar. Add egg yolks slowly. Add flour and sour cream alternately; add soda, salt to last bit of flour right before you add it to mixture. Fold in egg whites. Grease pan lightly with shortening. Bake at 325 degrees for about 1 1/2 hours or until straw comes out clean.

Serve with strawberries and whipped cream.

Variation
Add 2 tsp almond extract and sprinkle slivered almonds over the batter and bake as usual.

❦ Patti Brooks Krumnow

Strawberry Pie

- 1 qt berries
- 1 cup sugar
- 2 Tbls cornstarch
- 1/2 pt whipped cream
- baked 8-inch pie shell

Wash and hull berries. Put half in sauce pan with sugar and cornstarch. Cook over medium heat until clear. Cool some. Cut other berries in half and place in shell. Pour cooked berries over fresh fruit.

Serve with whipped cream. A few drops of red food coloring may be added to pie before chilling.

🌱 Christine Griffin

Sweet Potato Pie

- 3 cups mashed, cooked sweet potatoes
- 1 stick butter, softened to room temp.
- 2/3 cup sugar
- 1/3 cup firmly packed light brown sugar
- 3 eggs
- 1/4 tsp grated nutmeg
- 1 9-in. pie crust, unbaked

Preheat oven to 400 degrees. Combine sweet potatoes, butter, sugar, brown sugar, vanilla, eggs and nutmeg. Mix well. Pour into unbaked pie crust. Bake for 10 minutes. Reduce heat immediately to 350 degrees and continue baking for additional 35 minutes or until thin knife blade comes out clean when inserted into center of custard. Cool completely before slicing.

Put a dollop of whipped cream or cool whip on top.

Fruit Cobbler

- 1 stick margarine or butter
- 3/4 cups flour
- 1 cup sugar
- 2 tsp baking powder
- pinch salt
- 3/4 cup milk
- 2 cups sweetened fruit (peaches, berries, cherries etc.)

Put stick of oleo in baking dish or casserole in oven, set at 350 degrees, and let it melt. (Or melt in microwave.) Mix all ingredients except fruit and pour in casserole with melted butter. On top of this pour the sweetened fruit. Do not stir. Bake at 350 degrees until crusty.

Easy Fruit Cobbler

- 1/2 cup unsalted butter
- 1 cup all purpose flour
- 2 cups sugar, divided
- 1 Tbls baking powder
- pinch of salt
- 1 cup milk
- 4 cups fresh peach slices
- 1 Tbls lemon juice
- ground cinnamon or nutmeg

Melt butter on a 13 x 9 inch baking dish. Combine flour, 1 cup sugar, baking powder, and salt; add milk, stirring just until dry ingredients are moisten. Pour batter over butter. Do not stir. Bring remaining 1 cup sugar, peach slices, and lemon juice to a boil over high heat, stirring constantly; pour over batter. Do not stir. Sprinkle with cinnamon if desired. Bake at 375 degrees for 40-45 minutes or until golden brown, serve cobbler warm or cool. Makes 10 servings.

Super Sugar Cookies

- 1 cup butter
- 1 cup oil
- 1 cup sugar
- 1cup powdered sugar
- 2 eggs
- 1 tsp soda
- 4 cups flour
- 1 tsp salt
- 1 tsp vanilla
- 1 tsp cream of tartar
- granulated (regular ol') sugar for final step

In large bowl combine butter, oil and sugar; beat until creamy. Add powdered sugar, vanilla and eggs; mix well. In a small bowl, sift together flour, soda, cream of tartar and salt. Add to other ingredients and mix well. Cover dough and refrigerate at least 2 hours. Roll dough into 1-inch balls and roll in sugar. Flatten lightly on lightly greased cookie sheet. Bake at 350 degrees until light brown around the edges, about 12-15 minutes. Cool slightly before removing from cookie sheet. Makes about 100 cookies.

Wanda's Yellow Cake

- 1 cup Wesson oil
- 2 1/2 cups flour
- 1 1/2 tsp baking powder
- 1 cup milk
- 2 cups sugar
- 1 tsp vanilla
- 5 eggs

Cream oil and sugar, add eggs one at the time. Mix dry ingredients together (baking powder, flour) and add to batter. Add vanilla. Beat well. Pour in round cake pans and cook at 350 degrees for 20 minutes.

I found this recipe, handwritten in my mother's cookbook, but I don't know who Wanda is.

Fall in West Alabama

I worked for a company in Alabama as a community relations person. I called on large companies in an employee assistance capacity. In mid-October, I was sent over to West Alabama to call on a large lumber company.

West Alabama is the land of the big trees: pines, oaks, pecans, walnuts, hickories, and sycamores. The day was absolutely spectacular. It was one of those elegant Fall days: gentle breeze, temperature about 65, soft sunshine and incredibly gorgeous foliage. I had some favorite spiritual music playing on the tape deck and the beauty all around me had me in seventh heaven. I was driving about 50 miles an hour and as I rounded a curve up ahead a wild turkey ran across the road. I was thrilled... the only wild turkey I had ever seen was a picture of one on a bottle of whiskey. He obliged me by turning around and running back across the road so I could get a full view of him. I was full of appreciation that day for the beauty which surrounded me. What I also noticed was that the colors of the day would get incredibly bright and then fade back into their softness.

Daddy and his wife, Sara, had invited me over for supper that night and as I was thinking about that, my mind wandered. I realized that Daddy and I were getting along quite well. As a teen-ager, I had stood toe-to-toe with him in some awful rows. It seemed I was the only child who would not be bullied by him and was not phased by his blowing and going attempts to intimidate all around him. This day I realized at a very deep level that I had forgiven him for all that. Whatever had stood between me and him was gone. In the same instant, I realized that the little lump about the size of an acorn that was in the pit of my stomach all the time — the one that felt like unworthiness — was also gone. That day I got it on a gut level what the line in the Lord's Prayer means: "Forgive us our trespasses, as we forgive them that trespass against us." (Matthew 6:12)

Daddy and Sara each had their own easy chairs in the den. I always sat on the couch to the side of them. That night when I arrived for supper and we were catching up on the activities since we had last been together, Daddy got up from his easy chair and sat by me on the couch. He reached out and took my small hand and held it in his big hand.

Some barrier that we had become accustomed to had been removed that day in the Autumn of 1986 never to return. And each time I visited him he sat beside me on the couch and held my hand, until he died in September, 1989.

For he is our peace, who hath made one, and hath broken down the middle wall or partition between us. — **Ephesians 2:14**

Main Courses

Gift of the African Violet

Everything is a circle. You've often heard "as you give you receive." This is a circle that starts by giving; it curves around in a circle and becomes the receiving. So the act of giving and receiving is the same thing. Most of us have been trained that it is more blessed to give than receive. This is only partially correct.

When I was in about the sixth grade I went over to see a friend of mine. Barbara's mother raised exquisite African Violets. They were blooming in every window and on every shelf. They were a myriad of colors. I admired them profusely. Mrs. Smith said, "Patti, I would like for you to have one, pick the one you would like to have." I was embarrassed; I was afraid I might pick her prize violet and I was very much afraid that whichever one I took would die, so I just told her I couldn't possibly take one. She insisted, but I also as strongly insisted that I could not take one.

I told my mother about the offer when she came in that night and she really surprised me when she said I should have taken it. She said, "Patti, when you refused to take the plant, you deprived her of the pleasure of giving. Always accept a gift when it is sincerely offered." It had not occurred to me that I could have hurt her feelings by refusing. I had never looked at it from that angle and then it made perfect sense. When she gave and I received, we completed the circle. Both of us would have received great pleasure from this transaction.

A person who is generous in their giving is, in all likelihood, receiving more pleasure than the recipient. And because of their sincere generosity the universe is always returning their gifts ten-fold. An inability to give reflects a person who has an inability to love. Think of the old toothpaste ad, the one with the invisible shield between two people. If you have a shield in front of you, nothing can leave you and go out into the world. The shield also prevents anything from getting through back to you. You can see this person who has cut himself off from giving also has cut himself off from receiving as well.

So if you refuse the gift, remember you are short-circuiting the circle. To receive is as holy as to give.

For to him who has will more be given, and he will have abundance; but from him who has not, even what he has will be taken away. — **Matthew 13:12**
He that soweth sparingly shall reap also sparingly; and he which soweth bountifully shall reap bountifully. — **II Corinthians 9:6**

Mrs. Mullins Camp Stew

Takes 2 days to prepare and several soup kettles.

• 6-7 lb hen (save stock)
• 6 lb pork shoulder (save stock)
• 3 lbs boneless beef stew (save stock)
• 3 lbs Irish potatoes, creamed
• 3 cans tomatoes
• 2 packages frozen green lima beans
• 3 cans cream style corn
• A-1 sauce and Worcestershire sauce
    I'm guessing: 1 small bottle A-1 and Worscestershire.
• red pepper and salt to taste

Cook meat until it comes from bone and mix in large vessel with all above ingredients; add the creamed potatoes along with the stock from meat and stir constantly.

Note from my mother (Annette Brooks): "The above takes hours to cook. After mixing, simmer for an hour or longer. My uneducated guess it will serve 10 people at least."

Mrs. Mullins says in letter to "cook all day."

This is great to cook ahead and store in freezer bags. You traditionally eat this with plain white bread. It's an accompaniment to barbecue.

Mrs. Mullins Barbeque Sauce
This sauce is mixed with cooked shredded chicken. It's like a hash.
• 1 cup water
• 1 cup vinegar
• 2 Tbls salt
• 1 cup butter or margerine

Red pepper and black pepper to taste (this is hot); use lots.
Add some A-1 sauce if you like. Add little sugar to taste, cook it real low and thick. Pour over chicken hash and mix thoroughly.

Mrs. Mullins is Aunt Katherine Brooks' mother. Aunt Katherine was married to Joe Brooks, my Daddy's youngest brother.

Baked Chicken and Egg Noodles

- 1 fryer in pieces
- 1 stick butter
- 1 can cream of mushroom soup
- 1 can cream of chicken soup
- 1/2 soup can milk
- 1/2 soup can white wine
- 1 can mushrooms

Melt butter in large Pyrex baking dish. When melted, place chicken skin side down and bake about 20 minutes at 350 degrees. Turn over. Stir the soups, milk and wine together, add drained mushrooms. Stir well then pour over the chicken and bake for additional 25 minutes.

Serve with wide egg noodles.

Beef Brisket

- 1 brisket, salted and peppered
- 1 can beer
- 3 Tbls Worcestershire sauce
- 1 pkg onion soup mix

Mix beer, sauce and onion soup together. Wrap brisket in foil after trimming some fat off. Pour above mixture over brisket. Bake in pan overnight at 225 degrees, or bake any other time at 350 degrees until tender (at least 4 hours).

❤ Marge Zupko

Baked Pork Tenderloin

- 1/4 cup soy sauce
- 2 cloves garlic, pressed
- 2 slices green onions
- 3-4 slivers on ginger, pounded
- 1/4 cup white wine
- 1 pork tenderloin

Put all ingredients into a zip lock bag and marinate in refrigerator at least 3 hours. Remove from bag and bake at 350 degrees for about 35-40 min.

Barbecue Shrimp

- 6 1/4 lbs unpeeled medium sized shrimp
- 1/2 cup butter or margarine, melted
- 1/4 cup Worcestershire sauce
- 1/4 cup lemon juice
- 1 Tbls Old Bay seasoning
- 1 Tbls coarsely ground pepper
- 1-2 garlic cloves minced
- 1 Tbls Cajun seasoning
- 1 Tbls hot sauce

Peel shrimp and devein, if desired. Combine shrimp and remaining ingredients in a lightly greased large shallow roasting pan; toss to coat. Arrange shrimp in a single layer. Bake at 350 degrees for 15-20 minutes or until shrimp turn pink, stirring occasionally. Makes 25 servings.

God is Colorblind

I had a joyous visit with my grandson, Brooks, in Portland over Labor Day. Brooks will be a year old this month. I taught him to come kiss Ganmama, while I lay on the couch and read, and he toddled around investigating everything. Occasionally he would come over and rest his head on me or put his little mouth on my cheek and then go back to his busyness.

Several nights later we went out to eat. When we were getting the check he got really anxious to get out of the highchair so I let him down and he headed straight down the aisle to the end booth. A little boy about four years old was squatting down on the floor by his mother. Brooks toddled right up to him and gave him four slobbery kisses on his face. The little boy was smiling and turned to his mother who took her napkin and wiped his cheeks down. While he was standing Brooks kissed him three times on the stomach. The whole restaurant was oohing and aahing.

I used to watch this phenomenon all the time when I was a flight attendant. Children just love other children. And you know what else... they're color blind. I've seen white children hug and kiss black children and vice versa. I have seen Asian children kiss Indian children until the kisses surrounded the globe.

The affection shown by one child to another, even though they are strangers, tells me that we instinctively love each other and want to be friends. Have we been taught that anyone different from us is "bad" or "wrong"? We still have a chance at world peace with the development of our children. We also can start with ourselves and get rid of old beliefs and prejudices. We are all God's children made in his image and likeness. You know what? I believe that God is color blind too.

Let there be peace on earth and let it begin with me.

Beef Stroganoff

- 1 Tbls flour
- 1/2 tsp salt
- 1 lb top sirloin cut in 1/2 inch strips
- 2 Tbls butter
- 1 cup sliced fresh mushrooms
- 1/2 cup chopped onion
- 1 clove garlic, minced or pressed
- 2 Tbls butter
- 3 Tbls flour
- 1 Tbls tomato paste
- 1 can beef consomme
- 1 cup sour cream
- 2 Tbls sherry

Combine the flour and salt; roll meat strips in mixture. Melt 2 tablespoons butter in a skillet, add sirloin, and brown on all sides. Add mushrooms, onion and garlic; cook until onion is barely tender about 5 minutes. Remove meat and mushrooms temporarily from pan; melt 2 tablespoons butter in pan drippings and add 3 tablespoons flour, stirring to avoid lumps. Add tomato paste. Pour in consomme and cook, stirring constantly until mixture thickens. Return meat and mushrooms to skillet. (May be refrigerated at this point to finish and and serve later). Stir in sour cream and sherry; heat thoroughly, but don't boil.

Serve at once. This actually makes 3-4 servings, but once again the leftovers are great.

Serve with egg noodles or wild rice and a green salad.

Bernice's Cabbage Rolls (Holloopshi)

Remove core from cabbage with sharp knife. Cover cabbage with boiling water, and let it set until the leaves are soft. Drain the water off. Take the cabbage leaves off one at a time. Cut off any hard stems and centers.

Rice
Wash two cups of rice thoroughly. Add 1 teaspoon salt and 2 cups boiling water. Return to boil and then cut off and let the rice stand. Water is only partly absorbed.

Mix together:
- 1-2 lbs lean hamburger meat
- 1 lb package of sausage
- 1 egg
- onion to taste (at least 1 cup finely chopped)
- 3-4 tsps margarine
- rice

Season with salt and pepper. Cool.

Line bottom of soup kettle with outside leaves of the cabbage (this prevents sticking). Place several teaspoons of meat mixture in a cabbage leaf and roll up. Arrange the rolls on top of each other in the pan.

Mix in a bowl:
- 1 small can tomato paste
- 3 cans tomato juice instead of water
- 1/2 cup Parmesan cheese
- salt to taste
- dry parsley
- dry red and green bell pepper
- dry onion

Whip this mixture up with egg beater until thick.

Put about 2 inches of water or tomato juice in bottom of pot and simmer the cabbage rolls for about 1 hour. Add the tomato mixture the last hour of cooking.

❦ Bernice Hicks

Black Beans with Tomato Coulis

- 3 cans black beans, drained and rinsed
- 1/2 green pepper
- 1 bay Leaf
- cooking spray

Spray pan and then saute green pepper until tender, add beans and bay leaf and simmer about 20 minutes.

Serve over yellow or white rice and tomato coulis.

Fresh Tomato Coulis
- 4 medium to large tomatoes,chopped
- 1 clove garlic, pressed
- 3 Tbls chopped fresh cilantro
- 2 Tbls rice wine vinegar
- 1 tsp thyme
- 1 tsp freshly ground pepper

Combine in a bowl and refrigerate for at least 2 hours before serving.

Buffalo Wings

- 2 1/2 lbs chicken wings (about 12-15 wings)
- 4 Tbls Durkee's Red Hot Sauce (for hotter wings use up to 3/4 cups)
- 1/4 cup (1/2 stick) butter or margarine

No-Fry Method
Split wings at each joint and discard tips; pat dry. Place on baking pan. Bake wings,uncovered, at 325 degrees for 30 minutes. Remove from pan and place in container. Combine hot sauce and butter; pour over chicken wings. Cover and marinate in the refrigerator for at least 3 hours or overnight. Turn several times.

Before serving, broil wings 3-4 inches from heat for 5 minutes on each side, turning until brown and crisp and brushing often with reserved marinade. Brush with any remaining marinade just before serving.

Deep Fry Method (Original Buffalo Style)
Split wings at each joint and discard tips; pat dry. Deep fry at 400 degrees for 12 minutes until completely cooked and crispy. Drain. Combine hot sauce and butter. Toss wings in sauce to coat completely.

Makes 24 to 30 individual pieces. Serve with Roquefort dressing and celery sticks.

Cajun Casserole

- 2 Tbls salad oil or olive oil
- 1 cup raw rice
- 2 Tbls butter or oleo
- 1 onion, diced fine
- 1 clove garlic, pressed
- 1/2 green pepper
- 1 cup tomato juice
- 1 cup chicken broth or bouillon
- 1/2 tsp celery salt
- 1/2 tsp chili powder
- 1 tsp paprika
- 1 bay leaf
- 1 lb pork sausage

In a deep skillet, heat the oil. Add the rice and saute, stirring frequently, until the grains take on a golden color.

While tending this, melt the butter in another skillet and saute the onion, garlic and green pepper. Add the latter to the rice along with tomato juice, chicken broth, seasonings and bay leaf. Brown the sausage in the same skillet used to cook seasonings. Drain thoroughly on paper towels. Add to rice mixture. Cover skillet and cook until rice is tender (see how long your rice instructions say to cook the rice, and cook it that long.)

Grandfather Clock

Doing my errands one morning, I had occasion to go through the underpass at Ann St. and Interstate 85. Imagine my surprise as I got underneath to see a beautiful grandfather's clock on its back in the middle of the street just about covering the yellow line. I saw a pickup truck pulled over and several men were conferring and it appeared they had everything under control. As I drove away I remarked to myself at the time how much the clock looked like my grandmother's that had a prominent place in my Daddy's den.

My earliest recollections were at Grandmother Brooks' house in the first living room standing in front of the clock watching the pendulum gently swaying back and forth. I was too young to tell time so it was especially exciting if it started to chime in its deep mellow tones as I stood there. I also remember Grandmother with her hair down from its bun and she in her long sleeved night gown, from time to time at night opening the front of the clock and with the key she kept somewhere hidden from curious little hands she would wind the clock with long turns. My mother told me in a very secretive way that when Grandmama died, as they removed her body from the house, that the clock had stopped ticking.

Several weeks later I was over at Daddy's for supper and became aware of something in the room missing. It was a certain quietness. . . the clock was gone. "Daddy, where is the clock?" He looked sort of sheepish and Sara, his wife said, "Tell her, Dan."

Yes. That *was* my Grandmother's clock under the Ann St. overpass. Daddy, taking the clock in for its cleaning, had it in the back of his van, laying on a piece of carpet and tied in with fishing line. As he drove into the tunnel the clock was hiked in the air, but as he passed the middle the rear went down and the clock flew out of the back of the van like greased lightning.

The clock was a bit rattled by the experience, but being from good stock she rallied at the clock maker's and was back in fine fettle in several weeks.

The grand old clock has now moved on to my brother's home to be in a place of prominence there.

And I will put a new spirit within you. — **Ezekiel 11:19**

Blessings

Bean Patties

- 2 cups cooked dried beans
- 3 cups corn flakes
- 3 Tbls finely chopped onions
- 1 egg slightly beaten
- 1 Tbls catsup
- 3/4 tsp salt
- 1/4 tsp pepper
- 3 Tbls fat

Partially mash beans. Combine with finely crushed corn flakes, onion, egg, catsup, salt and pepper, mix well. Shape into patties. Fry in fat until browned, turning only once. Serve with catsup sauce. Makes 6 patties. May use left over navy, kidney or lima beans.

Catsup Sauce
- 3 Tbls butter or margarine
- 3 Tbls flour
- 3/4 tsp salt
- 1/8 tsp pepper
- 3 Tbls catsup
- 1 1/2 cups milk

Melt butter; add flour, salt pepper and catsup. Add milk slowly, stirring constantly over low heat until mixture thickens. Serve over Bean Patties.

I only buy Del Monte catsup.

Chicken and Dumplings

Before you read this recipe or prepare it, you are sworn to secrecy. Certainly no man should ever know that you did not slave for hours making dumplings from scratch.

- 1 3-4 lb fryer
- several stalks of celery
- 1 medium chopped onion

Cover chicken with Nature's Seasoning and a little sage. Bring to a boil, reduce heat and simmer until chicken leg is jiggly when you shake it. Remove chicken from the pot and let it cool. When cool enough to handle remove the chicken from the bones.

- One package flour tortillas, or about 12.

Cut tortillas into strips about an inch wide. Bring the chicken broth to a boil and return the chicken meat to the pot. Drop the tortilla strips into the slowly boiling broth. When all are in, push them down with a slotted spoon so they are completely submerged. Cover, reduce heat and simmer slowly about 20 minutes. Do not lift lid. Stand back and glory in the compliments.

Cheese Souffle

- 1 1/2 cups milk
- 1 lb butter
- 1 1/2 cups soft bread
- 3/4 tsp salt
- 1 tsp dry mustard
- 3 eggs (4, if small) beaten
- 1 3/4 cup grated extra sharp cheddar cheese

Pour scalded milk over bread crumbs. Let cool slightly, add other ingredients. Bake at 350 degrees for about an hour or until knife comes out clean. (May be assembled a day ahead. Remove from refrigerator 1 hour before baking.)

❦ Marci Griffin

Chicken Divan

- 1 lb fresh broccoli, cut in 1-inch pieces
- 1 lb carrots (optional) peeled and quartered lengthwise into 2-inch pieces
- 4 cups cooked chicken, cut into 1-inch pieces
      I prefer long strips
- 2 cans Healthy Request cream of chicken soup
- 1/2 cup sour cream
- 1/4 cup mayonnaise
- 1/4 cup plain yogurt (or sour cream)
- 2 Tbls lemon juice
- 1 1/2 -2 cups chicken broth
- 1 1/2 cups grated cheddar cheese
- 1 Tbls melted butter
- 1/2 cup slivered almonds

Microwave broccoli and carrots about 2-3 minutes to partially cook them. Combine soup, sour cream, mayonnaise, yogurt, lemon juice and chicken broth. Spray a 9 x 13 x 2 or 11 x 14 x 2 casserole dish with vegetable spray or butter the dish. Place chicken in casserole dish. Sprinkle with lemon pepper. Place vegetables on top. Cover with sauce. Top with cheese, melted butter and almonds. Bake at 350 degrees for 30 minutes. Serve over rice.

Another Chicken Divan

- 2 pkgs frozen broccoli
- cooked chicken (either a whole one or 4 breasts)
- 1 can cream of chicken soup
- 1/2 soup can mayonnaise
- juice of 1 lemon
- 1/2 soup can sherry
- Parmesan cheese
- seasoned bread crumbs

Run water over frozen broccoli to thaw; do not cook further. Spray Pam in the bottom of a baking dish. Layer broccoli and chicken. Mix soup, mayonnaise, lemon juice and sherry. Pour over broccoli and chicken. Sprinkle with Parmesan cheese and bread crumbs. Bake at 350 degrees for 30 minutes.

Chicken Country Captain

Dust chicken with flour. Brown chicken in part butter, part oil. Place in casserole dish.

Saute:
- 1 med onion
- 1 large green pepper
- 1-2 cloves garlic

Add:
- 2 med size cans tomatoes
Cook 10 minutes.

Stir in:
- 1 tsp salt
- 1 tsp each: curry powder, white pepper, thyme and parsley

Pour over chicken and sprinkle with 1/4 chopped almonds and 1 tablespoon currants.

Bake 350 degrees for 45 minutes. Serve with white rice and green salad.

Chicken Bombay

This is short-cut Chicken Country Captain.

• 2 lbs chicken pieces
• 2 Tbls shortening
• 1 can tomato soup
• 1/3 cup water
• 1/4 cup chopped onions
• 1 med clove garlic, minced
• 1 tsp curry powder
• 1/4 tsp thyme, crushed
• toasted slivered almonds, coconut, chutney, sliced green onions or raisins.

In skillet, brown chicken in shortening, pour off fat. Add soup, water, onion, garlic, curry and thyme. Cover, cook over low heat 45 minutes or until tender. Stir now and then.

Serve with a variety of the remaining ingredients. Serve with rice and salad.

Oh, Those River Monsters

My Daddy often told my daughters stories of when he was a little boy growing up in South Alabama on the Pea River.

One of their favorite stories was a day when he and some friends of his had been fishing early on a summer morning. The little boys were no older than eight years old and were leaving the river heading home for lunch. They were about the middle of the field when they looked back towards the river. Daddy said, "We saw this awful sight. There were these terrible looking monsters coming up out of the water. They had big horns and long green beards hanging around their mouths and they were looking straight at us. We started running as fast as our legs could carry us until we were over the barbed wire fence separating us from the monsters. Once safely on the other side we stopped long enough to look back to see if they were gaining on us. From this distant perspective we saw what they really were: three old cows who had been grazing along the river bank. As they lifted their heads out of the water, the long slimy green weeds they were eating looked for the world like green beards. Our knees went weak with relief. We weren't going to be monster lunch today." Of course we all convulsed with laughter.

My daughters often said how Granddaddy had such a wonderful time when he was a boy, much more fun than they had. I brought to their attention that this episode had been terrifying to the boys that morning. It was only with time and perspective that it had become so funny.

And so it goes with a lot of our life's lessons. Some are frightening at the time. However, if we have the faith to walk through our fears to the higher ground, we will be able to see how foolish most of our fears have been.

Luke 12:32 — *Fear not, little flock, for it is your Father's good pleasure to give you the kingdom.*

Chicken Rotel

- 1 12-oz. pkg vermicelli cooked
- 1 large hen or 6 chicken breasts cooked
- 2 cans Rotel tomatoes
- 1 big can English peas, drained
- 1 lb or less Velveeta cheese (lite)
- 1 large onion sauteed in oleo
- 1 large can mushrooms
- 1 stick oleo
- salt and pepper
- Season All
- 1 tsp garlic salt

Mix all together and cook at 350 degrees for 30 minutes.

❦ Juanita Krumnow

Don's Pot Roast

- 3 1/2-4 lb round or chuck roast
- 1 pouch onion soup mix
- 1 1/4 cups water
- 6 medium potatoes
- 6 carrots, cut into 2-inch pieces
- 2 tsp flour or corn starch

In a 6-quart Dutch Oven, in 2 tablespoons of hot oil, brown roast on all sides. Pour off fat. Sprinkle onion soup mix on top of roast. Add water. Cover. Bake 3 hours in 350-degree oven. Add vegetables and cook 45 minutes longer.

Remove roast and vegetables. Stir together flour or cornstarch with remaining 1/4 cup water until smooth. Gradually stir into soup mixture. Cook until mixture boils and thickens, stirring with a wire whisk. Pour a couple of teaspoons of Dale's, if you have it, over top of the roast.

❦ Don Krumnow

Chinese Chow

- 8 oz vermicelli
- 1 pint low fat sour cream
- 1 can sliced water chestnuts
- 2 lbs extra lean ground meat
- 1/2 cup chopped onions
- 2 cups chopped celery
- 1/4 cup pimento
- 1/2 cup green pepper
- 1 tsp salt
- Fat free cream of mushroom soup
- slivered almonds

Cook and drain vermicelli, toss with 1 pint of low fat sour cream. Add 1 teaspoon salt and 1 can sliced water chestnuts. Brown ground meat. Add, but do not cook: the onions, celery, pimento, and green pepper.

Sauce
- 1 cup fat-free cream of mushroom soup
- 1/4 cup soy sauce
- 1/2 cup water

Add sauce to meat. Pour vermicelli in bottom of dish. Add meat sauce on top. Sprinkle with slivered almonds. Bake uncovered 30 minutes at 325 degrees.

🐦 Juanita Krumnow

Cioppino

- 1 1/2 lb fresh fish fillets
- 1/2 lb shrimp, split and cleaned
- 12 squid, peeled and cleaned
- 12 hard shell clams
- 1/4 cup olive oil
- 1 medium green pepper, chopped
- 1 medium onion, chopped
- 1 clove garlic, chopped
- 4 ounces fresh mushrooms
- 1 can (1 lb, 12 oz) stewed tomatoes
     Try fresh tomatoes here.
- 2 cans (8 oz ea) tomato sauce
- 1 1/2 tsp seasoned salt
- 1/4 tsp pepper
- 2 cups water
- 1 cup dry white wine

Cut fillets and squid into 1-inch cubes. Cook green pepper, onion, garlic, and mushroom slices in olive oil until tender. Add tomatoes with liquid, tomato sauce, seasoned salt, pepper and water. Bring mixture to a boil, then reduce heat and simmer for 30 minutes. stirring occasionally. Add fish, shrimp, squid, clams and wine. Cover and simmer for 15 minutes, stirring occasionally. Serve in large soup bowls with chunks of heated French bread.

Clara Jane's Sausage Bake

- 2 lbs pork sausage, hot and mild, saute and drain
- 2 cups rice, uncooked
- 1 medium onion, chopped
- 4 Tbls soy sauce
- 1 cup celery, chopped
- 3 pkg cup-of-soup (chicken noodle)
- 4 cups water
- 1 cup slivered almonds
- 1/2 lb mushrooms, sliced
- bread crumbs

Saute and drain sausage on paper towels. Add rice, onion and celery, saute until rice is browned and onion and celery are partially cooked. Add soy sauce, soup, water. Stir in mushrooms. Cover top with almonds and bread crumbs and bake at 350 degrees about 35 minutes. Serves 6.

Clara Jane is unknown.

Cowboy Salad

- 1 can Ranch Style beans
- 1 cup grated cheese
- 1 tomato, peeled and cubed
- 1 small onion, sliced
- 2 cloves garlic, crushed
- 1 bottle Catalina dressing
- 1 head iceberg lettuce, shredded
- 1 medium bag original size corn chips

Drain beans and wash. Add cheese, tomato, onion, garlic and dressing. Marinate overnight in fridge. When ready to serve, add lettuce and corn chips and toss thoroughly.

Note: Do not put the chips or lettuce in too early. The lettuce will wilt and the chips will be soggy.

🌷 Ida Sing

Crab Cakes

- 1 lb claw crab meat
- 2 eggs
- 1/2 lb (1 stick) butter
- 1/2 tsp mustard
- 1/8 tsp black pepper
- pinch of cayenne pepper
- cooking oil
- bread crumbs

Mix crab meat, butter, seasoning and enough egg to mold into small flat cakes. Add bread crumbs. Fry until rich brown in frying pan or deep fry 380 degrees in well oiled frying basket. Very good with French fried potatoes. Cole slaw and tartar sauce.

Tartar Sauce
Combine and beat:
- 1 tsp mustard
- 1/8 tsp pepper
- 1 tsp confectioner's sugar
- 1/4 tsp salt
- onion juice or grated onion (about 1/2 tsp)
- 2 egg yolks
While beating this, slowly add 1/2 cup olive oil
- 3 Tbls vinegar (white)

When the sauce is thick add:
- 1 Tbls olives
- 1 Tbls capers
- 1 Tbls chopped cucumber pickle (dill)
- 1 Tbls chopped parsley

This will keep for weeks if you leave out the parsley.

Crab Imperial

- 1 lb backfin crab meat
- 3 Tbls flour
- 4 Tbls oil
- 2 cups milk
- 1 tsp dry mustard
- 1 Tbls capers
- 1 small jar diced pimentos
- 1 cup grated cheddar cheese
- salt and pepper to taste

Make a sauce of 3 tablespoons of flour sifted in 4 tablespoons of oil, cook on low heat and stir constantly. When mixed, add two cups of milk, stirring all the time. Salt and pepper to taste. Add 1 level teaspoon of dry mustard, 1 tablespoon of capers, 1 small can or jar of diced pimentos. Just before taking up, cut up or grate 1 cup of cheese, add, stir until completely melted, add crab meat.

Serve on rice.

❦ Annette Brooks

Crab Quiche

- pastry for 9-inch quiche pan or pie pan
- 1/2 cup mayonnaise
- 2 Tbls all purpose flour
- 2 eggs, beaten
- 1/2 cup milk
- 1 6-oz. package frozen crab meat, thawed and drained. (Also can use canned)
- 2 cups (8 oz) shredded Swiss cheese
- 1/3 cup chopped green onions
- fresh parsley sprigs (optional)
- tomato rose (optional)

Line a 9-inch quiche pan with pastry, and trim off excess around edge of pan. Place a piece of buttered aluminum foil, buttered side down, over pastry; gently press into pastry shell. This will keep the sides of the shell from collapsing. Cover foil with a layer of dried peas or beans. Bake at 400 degrees for 10 minutes. Remove foil and peas. Prick shell and bake additional 3-5 minutes or until light browned. Cool.

Combine mayonnaise, flour, eggs and milk; mix thoroughly. Stir in crab meat, cheese and onion. Spoon into a quiche shell and bake at 350 degrees for 30 minutes or until firm in center (insert knife: if it comes out clean its done). If desired, garnish with parsley and tomato rose.

Help

Daddy and Claude were going hunting. It was a gorgeous Fall day. They were about twelve years old and Claude was driving the new Ford. Claude's daddy owned the Ford dealership in Elba so Claude had his own car. Daddy was sitting on the hood of the car with his shotgun across his legs.

On the way out of town the boys got behind the school bus. There were some cute girls in the back with their faces pressed to the windows flirting with the boys. The boys were really into this when all of a sudden the Y in the road was upon them. With the girls, the flirting, and Claude's mind somewhere else he had last-minute confusion and couldn't remember where they were headed so with his mind on the girls he headed right instead of going to left, got rattled and went squarely up the middle. The car flipped throwing Daddy and his shotgun 20 feet in the air and it landed upside down. Daddy scrambled to his feet, looked around for Claude, and heard a quavery voice, "Help, help, Dan, help me." Daddy ran over to the car, looked all around it, and finally realized the voice was coming from underneath. He squatted down and there was Claude on all fours with the transmission braced upon his back. Daddy ran to the front of the car and lifted and struggled but couldn't budge the car. Then he ran to the back and lifted and tugged but the car didn't budge. In the meantime the quavery voice under the car was still calling. Daddy finally stuck his head under the car and appraising the situation said, "Claude get off your hands and knees and crawl out." Whereupon Claude flattened himself and wiggled out from under the car.

So often we lose our focus and forget momentarily where we're going. This is when confusion happens and we end up going up the middle instead of to the right or left. When we keep our attention focused on what we are doing and where we are going the powers of the universe rush in to move us swiftly to our destination. Without a map and a destination marked we flounder here and there. Sit down for an hour or two and write down what you want to accomplish. Revise it for several days until you are really focused on what you want to accomplish. This is what's meant by your eye being the lamp of your body (focused). If I have a major goal to accomplish I browse through magazines and cut out pictures that fit the goal and glue them on a piece of poster paper. I always put a religious symbol on the poster as well, like a cross or a picture of Jesus or a church. This is my visible way of saying, "With God's help," and that my motives are pure. Tack your completed poster to the back of your bedroom door or where you can see it several times a day. These are your goals in pictures. It keeps you focused on where you're going. When the goals have been met, make a new poster. This way you always know where you're going. You are not likely to end up upside down in the middle of the Y.

Luke 11:34-36 — *Your eye is the lamp of our body; when your eye is sound, your whole body is full of light; but when it is not sound, your body is full of darkness. Therefore be careful lest the light in you be darkness. If then your whole body is full of light, having no part dark, it will be wholly bright, as when a lamp with rays gives you light.*

Eggs RVC

- butter
- 6 eggs
- 1 1/2 milk

Butter dish. Butter de-crusted bread slices and place in casserole dish butter side down. Cover with slices of Velveeta or cheddar. Butter bread again and place butter side up. Beat eggs and milk until frothy and pour over bread mixture. Place in refrigerator, covered, overnight.

Take out of refrigerator an hour before baking. Put uncovered casserole dish in pan of water and bake 325-350 degrees until firm and brown. Allow 1 1/2 hours.

Place crumbled bacon on top. Put slice of Canadian Bacon on top of toasted English muffin. Place slice of casserole on top of bacon and muffin.

This is a great Sunday brunch dish.

Serve with garlic-cheese grits and buttered English Muffins. Have lots of preserves and jellies.

Bob Christian used to make this for us when we were flying (for Delta). Us is Lynn Greer, Carole Ann Tessier and me. Bob worked for Delta then in the public relations department. He was a former sports writer for the Atlanta Constitution.

Curried Chicken

- 1- 4 1/2 to 6 lb chicken
- 3 cups water
- 2 1/2 tsp salt
- 1/4 tsp pepper
- 1 medium onion, finely chopped
- 1 1/2 Tbls chopped parsley
- 1 apple, peeled and finely chopped
- 6 Tbls flour
- 3/4 cup evaporated milk
- 1 Tbls curry powder
- 1/4 tsp ginger

Place chicken in water add ingredients through apple. Simmer until chicken is ready to fall from bones. Remove chicken from stock and remove from bone in large pieces. Save 3 cups broth. Mix flour and 3 tablespoons margarine and 3 tablespoons broth. Stir in bottom of kettle until thick. Add evaporated milk and blend until smooth, add broth stirring constantly. Add curry and ginger. Cook stirring constantly, until thickened. Add chicken; heat to serving temp.

Serve with rice and curry condiments: coconut, chutney, peanuts and raisins.

Curry in a Hurry

- curry chicken (see below)
- rice with almonds and raisins
        I would toast the almonds first.
- yogurt with cucumbers
- vanilla ice cream with coconut and crushed pineapple

Curry Chicken
- 1 lb chicken breasts, boneless and skinless
- salt and pepper to taste
- 3 Tbls butter
- 1 medium onion
- 1 garlic clove
- 1 1/2 cups chicken broth
- 2 Tbls curry powder, or to taste
- 1/4 tsp powdered ginger
        I prefer fresh grated: keep it frozen and grate it.
- 2 Tbls flour
- 1 apple cored, peeled and chopped
- 1 medium to large banana, diced
- garnish: chopped peanuts

Cut chicken breasts into 1-inch cubes and sprinkle with salt and pepper. In a skillet, over medium heat, cook chicken in 2 tablespoons of butter until it loses its pink color (about 5 minutes); remove from pan. Add remaining butter to skillet and sauté onion and garlic until just browned. Add chicken broth gradually with curry powder, ginger and flour; stir to combine. Add apple, banana, and chicken. Cover and simmer 10 to 15 minutes.

Serve garnished with peanuts.

For dessert, serve vanilla ice cream topped with shredded coconut and canned crushed pineapple.

Fajitas

- 1/3 cup tomato paste
- 1 1/4 cups strong brewed coffee
- 1/2 cup Worcestershire
- 1 Tbls sugar
- 2 tsp red pepper
- 1 tsp black pepper
- 3 Tbls lime juice
- 1 Tbls light olive oil
- 2 (1 1/2 lb) flank steaks
- 24 flour tortillas
- pico de gallo (see below)

Garnishes
- Cilantro sprigs, lime wedges, Chile peppers, avocado slices.

Combine tomato paste and next seven ingredients in a zip-lock bag and add steaks. Chill 8 hours turning the meat often. Remove steaks and reserve the marinade (marinade should never be used as is, it has to be thoroughly heated to kill the bacteria). Cook steaks over hot coals about 6 minutes on each side. Bring marinade to a boil in a skillet; boil 10-15 minutes or until reduced to 1 cup. Cut steaks diagonally across the grain.

Place steak down center of tortillas; drizzle with marinade, and top with Pico. Roll up and serve immediately.

Pico de Gallo
- 2 tomatoes, chopped
- 1/2 cup chopped onion
- 1/2 cup fresh cilantro
- 2 serrano chile peppers, chopped
- 2 Tbls olive oil
- 1-2 tsp lemon juice
- 1/4 tsp salt
- 1/4 tsp pepper

Combine all ingredients; chill. Makes1 1/3 cups.

French Ham and Cheese Fondue

- 3 cups cubed French bread (about 1/2 loaf)
- 3 cups cooked cubed ham
- 1/2 lb cheddar cheese, cut in 1 inch cubes
- 3 Tbls flour
- 1 Tbls dry mustard
- 3 Tbls melted butter or margarine
- 4 eggs
- 3 cups milk
- few drops Tabasco seasoning

Make a layer of one-third of the bread, ham and cheese cubes in a buttered, straight-side, 8-cup baking dish. Mix flour and mustard in a cup. Sprinkle about 1 tablespoon over layer; drizzle 1 tablespoon melted butter or margarine over. Repeat with remaining bread, ham, cheese, flour mixture and butter or margarine to make two more layers. Beat eggs with milk and Tabasco until light in medium size bowl; pour over layers in baking dish. Cover; chill at least 4 hours, or even overnight. Bake uncovered in moderate oven, 350 degrees, for 1 hour or until puffed and brown.

It's a flashy make-ahead, for the secret to its handsome puffiness is long chilling before baking. Makes 6 servings.

🐦 Marci Dillon Griffin

Marci says: "This is from a magazine about 30 years old. I used to cook it and believe me it is delicious. You can double it and I used it for supper parties."

If She Can Trust

Right before I was accepted into the seminary I was having some real problems, trying to figure out how and why would I possibly want to actually quit a $40,000 a year job to go back to school and probably starve for the next two years. After all, I was 48 years old and should be thinking more about donating to my retirement account.

One Sunday about this time, I approached my minister with this dilemma and said, "Jerry, I know I'm going to the seminary but I just don't think I have enough faith that I'll be provided for. I'm really scared." My wise Reverend Jerry said, "Patti, you have all the faith you need. What you have to work on is trust."

I drove away from church thinking about the differences in these two words. I had stopped at the light at Five Points. This was indeed an intersection with five cross streets but to further confuse it on one side there were huge holes dug to accommodate the new storm sewer system in Birmingham. As I looked up at my light, a girl proceeded to cross the street with a seeing-eye dog leading her. He watched for traffic from all sides and then led her safely along side of those monstrous holes.

You know, I got it! If she can trust her life to that dog, then I could certainly trust mine to God. I cried for the next 15 miles.

That was seven years ago. I got through school and then out in the real world to start a church in a strange town from scratch. And do you know, I have never missed a meal. I've always had a roof over my head and everything I need.

Today, make a decision. Write a note and put it on your mirror in the bathroom as a reminder. "'Patti, Let me do it today.' Love, GOD."

Ground Beef Vegetable Casserole

Fry and cut up three strips of bacon. Add 1 lb hamburger and 2 large chopped onions. Add 1/4 cup light soy sauce, 1/4 teaspoon pepper and 1/2 cup water.

Add vegetables in layers:
- 2 sliced potatoes
- 1 sliced green pepper
- 2 sliced tomatoes
- 3 stalks celery
- 2 cups chopped cabbage

Cover and cook over high heat 1 minute. Reduce and cook slowly 15 minutes or until the vegetables are wilted.

This is a great meal in a dish. Serve with corn bread.

Chicken and Sausage Gumbo

- 4-5 chicken breasts
- 2 onions
- 4 ribs celery
- 1 green pepper
- 3 cloves garlic
- 1 bay leaf
- 1/2 tsp thyme
- 1/4 tsp marjoram
- 1 cup minced parsley
- 1 lb sausage
- 1 1/2 lbs fresh slice okra or 1 16-oz. bag frozen okra

Brown chicken breasts (boneless and skinned) in small amount of oil. Remove chicken. Chop 2 onions, 4 ribs celery, 1 green pepper, 3 cloves garlic. Add to skillet that chicken was browned in. In a large pot, add 3 quarts water. Heat until medium warm. Add chicken and vegetables. Add spices.

In meantime, slice 1 lb sausage into 1/4-inch thick slices and bake until all grease is out. Drain and add to gumbo, salt and pepper to taste.

Roux
In a heavy skillet or iron frying pan brown 2 parts flour to one part oil and cook until rich dark brown. Add roux to gumbo, stirring well. Add 1 1/2 lbs fresh sliced okra or 1 16-oz. bag frozen sliced okra.

Seafood Gumbo
Omit chicken and sausage and add one at a time: 1 1/12 lb shrimp,1 lb crabmeat,1 pint oysters. Do not overcook the seafood. Heat thoroughly until shrimp is pink, then add oysters until they shrivel, and then add crabmeat.

❦ Marge Zupko

King Crab Paella

- 2 whole chicken breasts
- 1/3 cup olive oil
- 1 large green pepper, seeded and chopped
- 1 large onion, chopped
- 2 5-oz. packages yellow rice mix
- 4 cups chicken broth or chicken bouillon
- 2 packages frozen king crab legs, defrosted and drained
- 1 10-oz. package frozen green peas
- 12 littleneck clams or mussels

Bone the chicken and cut each whole breast into 6 pieces. Heat the olive oil in a large heavy skillet and saute the chicken, green pepper and onion until golden brown. Stir in yellow rice mix. Saute for 5 minutes, add the chicken broth, cover and cook over low heat, stirring occasionally, until the rice is tender. Add the crab legs, pimento and peas. Place the scrubbed clams or mussels on top of the rice mixture. Cover and let simmer until the clam or mussels shells open. Serve immediately. Serves 6.

Always throw away the shells that don't pop open (they're bad).

Grandma Smith's Pork Chops and Sauerkraut

Brown chops on both sides, take out of pan and drain off all fat. Cut up two large onions (and green peppers if desired) add more butter on top of onions, with 1 teaspoon of paprika and let it melt, add kraut and stir. Put half of the kraut mixture in bottom of the baking dish, place chops on top, spoon rest of mixture on top.

Cover and put in 325-degree oven for about 1 hour until chops are tender. Delicious.

🌱 Mary Emily Murray Smith

King Ranch Chicken

- 4 skinned and boned chicken breasts
- 1/4 tsp salt
- 2 Tbls butter
- 1 green pepper, chopped
- 1 medium onion, chopped
- 2 10-oz. cans Rotel tomatoes
- 1 can cream of mushroom soup
- 1 can cream of chicken soup
- 12 6-in. corn tortillas, cut into quarters
- 2 cups 8-oz. shredded cheddar cheese

Bake salt and peppered chicken at 375 degrees for 30 minutes until done. Cool. Remove chicken from the bone and cut into 1-inch pieces. Melt butter in a large skillet over medium heat. Add chopped pepper and onion, and cook, stirring mixture constantly until vegetables are crisp-tender. Remove from heat and stir in chicken, tomatoes, and soups. Place one third of tortilla quarters in bottom of a lightly greased 13 x 9 x 2 baking dish; top with 1/3 of chicken mixture, and sprinkle evenly with 2/3 cup shredded Cheddar cheese. Repeat layers twice, reserving remaining 2/3 cheese.

Bake at 350 degrees for 35 minutes; sprinkle with reserved cheddar cheese and bake 5 additional minutes, let stand 5 minutes before serving. Serves 6-8.

Leg of Lamb

- 1 6-lb leg of lamb
- 1 garlic clove, crushed
- 1 1/4 tsp salt
- 1 tsp ground pepper
- 2 Tbls olive oil
- 1 tsp marjoram
- 1 tsp rosemary
- 1 tsp thyme
- 2 Tbls flour
- 1 cup dry white wine
- 1 cup water

Place lamb in a shallow roasting pan without a rack. Crush garlic in a small bowl with salt and pepper. Mix with olive oil and rub on lamb with fingers. Sprinkle roast with spices and flour. Pour wine and water in pan with lamb. (not on the lamb) Roast at 325 degrees for 2 1/2 -3 hours, basting every 25-30 minutes. Serves 6.

Serve with Uncle Ben's Wild Rice and frozen baby lima beans with some okra in them.

Patti's Lamb-Barley Soup

- lamb bones from leftover leg of lamb or leg bones from grocery
- 1 1/2 qts water
- 1 can stewed tomatoes
- 3/4 cup pearl barley, washed until water is no longer cloudy
- 1 tsp salt
- 1 tsp black pepper
- carrots
- 1 can lima beans or half pkg frozen green baby limas
- leftover wild rice or Uncle Ben's wild rice mix
- any leftover vegetables in refrigerator such as carrots, onions, squash, zucchini

Bring water, lamb-bones, tomatoes and barley to a boil. Add salt and pepper and reduce heat and simmer about an hour. Add rice, limas, carrots, and any chopped vegetables, simmer for another 30 minutes. Serve with corn bread or some nice bakery bread with butter.

Lentil and Bulgur Pilaf
With Green and Yellow Squash

- 4 cups reduced-sodium chicken broth, defatted
- 1 cup bulgur, medium or coarse grain
- 1 cup brown lentils, rinsed
- 1 onion, chopped
- 1 bay leaf
- 1 tsp salt, plus more to taste
- 1/2 tsp ground allspice
- 1/4 tsp freshly ground black pepper, more to taste
- 1 Tbls fresh lemon juice
- 1 Tbls olive oil
- 1 small zucchini, halved lengthwise and cut into 1/4-inch thick slices
- 1 clove garlic, minced
- 1 tsp grated lemon zest (grated lemon rind)
- 1 Tbls finely chopped fresh parsley
- 1 Tbls finely chopped fresh cilantro
- lemon wedges for garnish

In a 3 quart saucepan, combine broth, bulgur, lentils, onion, bay leaf, 1 teaspoon salt, allspice and 1/4 teaspoon pepper and bring to a boil over medium heat. Reduce heat to low, cover, and cook until liquid is absorbed and bulgur and lentils are tender, about 35 minutes. Remove pilaf from heat and stir in lemon juice.

Meanwhile, in a non stick skillet, heat oil over medium heat. Add zucchini, squash, garlic, and lemon zest; saute for 5 minutes. Stir in parsley and cilantro. Taste to adjust seasonings. Stir into pilaf. Serve hot with lemon wedges.
Makes 8 cups, for 6 servings.

This is wonderful!

London Broil

- 1 Tbls flour
- 1/2 tsp salt
- flank steak
- 2 Tbls butter
- 1 cup sliced fresh mushrooms
- 1/2 cup chopped onion
- 1 clove garlic, minced or pressed
- 2 Tbls butter
- 3 Tbls flour
- 1 Tbls tomato paste
- 1 can beef consomme
- 2 Tbls sherry

Combine the flour and salt; melt 2 tablespoons of butter in a skillet. Cook until light brown. Add mushrooms, onion and garlic; cook until onion is barely tender about 5 minutes. Remove mushrooms temporarily from pan; melt 2 tablespoons butter in pan drippings and add 3 tablespoons flour, stirring to avoid lumps. Add tomato paste. Pour in consomme and cook, stirring constantly until mixture thickens. (May be refrigerated at this point to finish and serve later.) Stir in sherry; heat thoroughly but don't boil.

In the meantime, salt and pepper the flank steak and broil under broiler for 7 minutes. Remove to serving platter. Slice across the grain at an angle. Pour sauce over the London Broil.

Serve at once. This actually makes 3-4 servings but once again the leftovers are great.

Serve with roasted potatoes or wild rice and a green salad.

Jack Hammer

When I die I would like to be cremated and have my ashes sprinkled in the bluebonnets. I have told my children this for years and when they asked where in the bluebonnets. I told them I didn't care, Interstate 10 would be just fine. But God is so good to me. Don and I are building a beautiful home on Hwy 20 between Fentress and Seguin. The house sits on the hill overlooking a 180-degree vista of at least 40 miles and close up it overlooks the small pond we've put in. At this stage in the game, the pond only has maybe six feet of water at the deepest. The kildees have found it as well as seven kerplunks that I've identified as bull frogs of varying sizes. A perfect place to have my ashes spread. But I'm detouring off the subject. If I had a tombstone, which I probably won't, I would want my epitaph to read: "She didn't die curious." Meaning of course that anything I have some curiosity about I intend to satisfy before I pass on.

One of the things that I always had great curiosity about was a jack hammer. That's right. All 5-foot-2-inches and105 pounds of me wanted to work one of those things!

When I was a flight attendant for Delta Airlines, back in the dark ages before the advent of jets, I flew a twin engine Convair 440 from Atlanta to Detroit. It was a puddle jumper with at least six stops along the way. The crew spent the night in Detroit and then headed out again very early the next morning. On one of these mornings, I met the rest of the crew for breakfast at a nearby Waffle House. Wouldn't you know it: a crew was breaking up the street in front of the restaurant with jack hammers.

There I was in my Edith Head designed beige uniform with the coral ascot around my neck and that little hat with the Delta widget on the side (if we were caught without that hat pinned to our heads, we were suspended for 10 days without pay), crisp and clean ready for my 10-hour day of flying. A strange glazed look came over my face, I excused myself from the table and walked outside and tapped this big burly construction worker on his back. We did hand motions until he got my message that I would like to work that thing. He held me and the jackhammer for about 30 seconds and all the teeth in my head were jarred loose and then he let me go. I adjusted my hat back on straight, went back to my table, sat down and took another bite of eggs.

I was one satisfied female. Do I ever want to do that again. I don't think so. But I won't die curious.

Macaroni and Cheese

- 1 package elbow macaroni
- 1 lb sharp cheddar cheese
- 1 can mushroom soup mix
- 2 Tbls grated onion

Cook macaroni until just tender. Drain, rinse and place in casserole dish. Stir in cubed cheese, soup, and grated onion. Bake at 350 degrees for about 30 minutes. Stir before serving. Will serve 6 hungry people.

Serve with whole broiled tomatos and salad.

Mediterranean Tuna and Macaroni Salad

- !/2 lb small shell macaroni
- 1/4 cup olive oil
- 3 Tbls lemon juice
- 4 Tbls balsamic vinegar
- 1 tsp salt
- 1/2 tsp pepper
- 1 Tbls fresh oregano, chopped
- 1 can water packed tuna, drained
- 1/2 cup chopped onion (optional)
- 1 cup chopped Roma or homegrown tomatoes
- 3 Tbls capers
- 3 Tbls chopped salad olives
- 1/2 yellow or red bell pepper
- 1/4 cup fresh parsley (optional)

Cook shells according to directions. Drain and rinse in cold water to remove heat. In large bowl combine olive oil, lemon juice, vinegar, salt and pepper and whisk well. Add oregano, tomatoes, capers and olives (onions and parsley) and allow to marinate. When macaroni is cool, add macaroni and tuna and stir thoroughly. Serves 3.

Mama's Ribs and Sauerkraut

- package of baby back or small pork ribs
- 1 large jar or can of sauerkraut, drained
- 1 small can of V-8. Not the big one and not the little single size
- 2 tsp caraway seeds
- 2 apples, chopped, or package of dried apples
- 1/2 cup brown sugar

Lay ribs across the bottom of a soup kettle. Pour drained Kraut on top. Sprinkle with caraway seed, pour in chopped or dried apples, sprinkle brown sugar over top. Pour V-8 over the top of all. Cover and simmer for 1 1/2 hours.

❦ Patti Brooks Krumnow

Meat Loaf

- 1 lb lean meat, preferably ground round
- 1/2 small onion, chopped fine
- 1 large squirt catsup (about 3 Tbls)
- 1 medium squirt French's mustard (about 2 Tbls)
- salt and pepper

Mix together with bare hands until well mixed. Shape into a loaf and pat down in loaf pan. Check every 15 minutes or so and pour off any accumulated fat. Bake at 350 degrees for about 45 minutes. About 15 minutes before done cover top with catsup and return to oven.

Shrimp Casserole

Sauté in butter:
- 1/4 cup onion
- 1/2 green pepper
- 1/2 cup celery

Add ham and shrimp:
- 1 4 1/2-oz. can deviled ham
- 2 cans shrimp

In measuring cup drain mushrooms, and tomatoes, add bouillon to make 2 cups liquid.

- 1 can mushrooms
- 1 can tomatoes
- 1 can bouillon or consomme
- 1/2 tsp sugar
- 1/2 tsp chili powder
- 1/2 tsp tabasco
- 1 cup uncooked rice
- 1 8-oz. can peas drained
    I prefer frozen green peas added at the last minute.

Add seasonings and rice. Cook covered 20 minutes at 350 degrees. Add tomatoes, mushrooms and peas. Stir and heat through.

🍂 Mary Jane Orsborn

New Orleans Red Beans and Rice

• 1 lb dried red kidney beans
• 2/3 cup each chopped onion, celery, green pepper
• 2 tsp minced garlic
• 1/2 cup oil
• 2 bay leaves
• 2 tsp salt
• 2 tsp Hungarian paprika
• 1 tsp thyme
• 1/2 tsp oregano
• 1/4 tsp red pepper
• 1/2 cup fresh parsley
• 1 lb andouille sausage or smoked Polish sausage, cut into 1-inch pieces.

Wash beans, place in a 6 quart Dutch oven. Cover with 3 inches of water. Bring to a boil, then reduce heat to medium. Melt butter or using oil, add onion, celery, green pepper and garlic and sauté until tender. Stir into beans. Add more water if necessary. Add all other ingredients to beans except sausage. Bake sausage in oven at 350 degrees for about 30 minutes. Drain and add to beans, continue cooking until tender. Serve over rice.

Oven Rice
• 1 1/2 cups uncooked rice
• 2 1/2 cups chicken broth
• 2 Tbls finely chopped celery, onion and green pepper
• 1 1/2 Tbls butter
• 1/2 tsp salt
• dash of pepper
• 1/4 tsp garlic powder

Combine all ingredients in a 2-quart baking dish, stirring well. Cover and bake at 350 degrees for 1 hour or until all liquid is absorbed. 6 servings.

❦ Marge Zupko

Quick Creole Shrimp

- 1 lb shrimp, boiled
- hot sauce to taste
- 1 cup onion,chopped
- 1 tsp salt
- 1 cup chopped green pepper
- 1/2 tsp pepper
- 1 cup chopped celery
- 1 qt fresh tomatoes, chopped
- 2 Tbls bacon drippings
- Rice
- 1 Tbls Worcestershire sauce

Shell and devein shrimp; cut in half if too large. Sauté shrimp, onion, pepper, and celery in bacon drippings. Add other ingredients except rice and put in a 2 1/2 quart baking dish., Bake at 450 degrees for about 15 minutes. Yields 6 servings.

Serve over cooked rice.

Deviled Crab

- 1/2 lb crab meat
- 1/2 cup milk or cream
- 1 Tbls flour
- 1 tsp lemon juice
- 1/2 tsp Worcestershire sauce
- 1 Tbls butter
- 1 egg yolk
- 1 tsp grated onion
- 1/2 cup finely buttered bread crumbs
- 1/2 tsp mustard, red pepper and salt to taste
- 1 Tbls red and green pepper, finely chopped

Melt butter, stir in flour; add milk and cook until it thickens. Add slightly beaten egg yolk and crab meat. Add seasonings and cook 3 minutes. Stir in onion, lemon juice and red and green peppers. Fill crab shell with mixture. Sprinkle with bread crumbs. Bake in hot oven until top is browned (about 400 degrees). Serves 4.

Another Deviled Crab

- 4 Tbls butter
- 1 medium onion, finely diced
- 2 large mushrooms, finely chopped
- 1/2 green pepper, finely chopped
- 1/4 tsp salt
- 1/2 tsp dry mustard
- 1/8 tsp black pepper
- 1 Tbls Worcestershire Sauce
- dash Tabasco
- 2 Tbls flour
- 1 cup hot milk
- 1 cup hot clam broth (or bottled clam juice)
- yolks of 2 eggs
- 1 lb lump crab meat

Sauté onion, mushrooms and green pepper in butter. Add salt, pepper, dry mustard, Worcestershire sauce and Tabasco. Then add flour, hot milk, hot clam broth and the well-beaten egg yolks and cook together for 10 minutes. Add crabmeat and cook for five minutes more. Remove from fire and pile into large chowder clam shells or individual oven proof ramekins. Dust with cracker meal and brush tops with melted butter. Bake in preheated 400-degree oven till brown on top.

❦ Annette Brooks

Joe's A-

When we entered Unity Ministerial School we had to maintain a B+ average for the two years we were there. Our first paper was on a comparison of the Creation Stories in Genesis. Our Bible teacher was Frank Guidici, a great Bible scholar, a masterful teacher, and one of the hardest graders in the school. We all waited with fear and trepidation the morning our papers were returned. I got a B+ which I was quite pleased with given the circumstances. It was really amazing to watch my classmates with their papers. It was like a big conspiracy. Nobody told their grades. Those papers went into briefcases not to come out again. I thought it was a strange reaction although I didn't broadcast my grade either, and nobody sidled up and asked me what I got on my paper. Strange reaction.

It was only recently that one of my classmates confided to me that he had gotten an A- on his paper and had gone back to his dorm room and cried and hyperventilated for half the afternoon.

As the first year passed, I realized that it didn't matter what I got on a paper or a test, I was never happy with it. And then I got it. I was telling myself that no matter how good I did, it wasn't good enough. That was the same reaction Joe had had with his A-. After that "Ah-ha" experience, I got off my case. As long as I maintained a B+ average in each class that was fine with me. Grades set up competition which is deadly for self-esteem. The competition should only be from within. Did I do the best that I could do? If the answer is yes, then a C is a good grade. If I didn't do my best and I got a B+, that isn't good enough because I didn't give it my best shot.

We are each one of a kind. We each have talents and abilities which are unique to us that the world needs. We don't need to be looking at others to see how well or poorly they're doing and then comparing ourselves to that. We need to be looking within and discovering our own unequaled self.

We each represent a part of God that He needs here on Earth to fulfill His purpose. Are you fulfilling yours?

Jeremiah 29:11 — *For I know the plans I have for you, says the Lord, plans for welfare and not for evil, to give you a future and a hope.*

Picadillo (Cuban)

- 1 lb ground beef
- 2-3 onions chopped
- 3-4 gloves garlic
- 1 green pepper chopped
- 1 can chopped tomatoes
- 1 can Rotel chopped tomatoes
- 1-2 med. boiled potatoes, chopped
- 1/2-3/4 cup raisins
- 1/2-3/4 cup white wine
- 1/2 cup diced pimento- stuffed olives
- salt and pepper to taste, also garlic powder

Break up and fry beef. When red is just gone add onions and garlic. Cook together until onions begin to be transparent. Add all other ingredients and cook over medium-low heat for 20-30 minutes. Do not overcook.

Serve over rice w/green salad, garlic bread and white wine.

❦ James W. Horne III
     Son of Billie Creech Horne.

Polynesian Chicken

- 1 41/2-6 lb chicken cut in serving pieces
- 3 cups water
- 1 onion, slices
- 2 celery tops
- 2 bay leaves
- 2 1/2 tsp salt
- 10 peppercorns

Put together in a large pot and simmer until meat is ready to fall from the bones, about 1 hour. Save the stock for chicken and dumplings.

Polynesian Chicken
- 1 can pineapple chunks
- 2 Tbls soy sauce
- 1 1/2 cups chicken broth
- 2 Tbls cornstarch
- large pieces cooked chicken
- 1 cup diagonally cut celery
- 2 medium tomatoes, cut in wedges
- 1 green pepper, thinly sliced and halved
- slivered toasted almonds
- cooked rice

Drain pineapple, combine syrup, soy sauce, broth and cornstarch in saucepan. Blend until smooth. Place over medium heat, stirring constantly, until thickened. Add chicken, celery tomatoes and green peppers. Cover and simmer 15 minutes.

Serve over cooked rice. Garnish with toasted almonds .

Potpourri de Poulet

- 2 cups cooked chicken, cubed
- 2 cups celery, chopped
- 1/2 cup toasted almonds, chopped
- 1/2 tsp salt
- 2 Tbls onion, grated
- 1/2 cup bell pepper, diced
- 1/2 cup mayonnaise
- 2 Tbls pimento dice
- 2 Tbls lemon juice
- 1/2 cup cream of chicken soup
- 1/2 cup American cheese, grated
- 3 cups potato chips, crushed

Preheat oven to 350 degrees. Grease 1 1/2 quart casserole. Combine all ingredients except cheese and potato chips. Toss lightly and place in greased casserole. Spread cheese and potato chips on top. Bake uncovered until heated through and browned on top. Garnish with parsley. Serves 6.

🍋 Marci Griffin

Rainbow Trout with Caper Sauce

- 6 1/2 lbs rainbow trout, however you get it, 6 1/2 lb fish or 6 1/2 lb filets
- 3/4 cup dry white wine
- 3/4 cup well seasoned chicken stock
- 1/2 tsp peppercorns
- 1 bay leaf
- salt
- 4 Tbls butter
- 1/3 cup flour
- 1 1/2 cup hot milk
- 1/4 cup chopped capers
- 2 Tbls freshly grated Parmesan cheese

Combine the wine, chicken stock, peppercorns and bay leaf in a large skillet and simmer, covered, while the fish are defrosting. Sprinkle 1/4 teaspoon salt in the cavity of each trout and place the fish in the bubbling liquid. Simmer for 15-20 minutes of until the fins loosen easily from the body of the fish.

Remove the fish, cool them for a few minutes before skinning and filleting them. Place the filets slightly overlapping in a well-buttered shallow oven-to-table dish.

Strain the stock in which the fish cooked, measure it and add water, if necessary to make 1 1/2 cup liquid. Melt the butter in a saucepan over medium heat, blend the flour and gradually add the fish stock and milk. Blend, stirring constantly until the sauce is thickened and smooth. Remove from the heat and add the capers and more salt if necessary. Spoon over the fish and sprinkle the Parmesan cheese on top. Bake in a 375-degree oven for 20 minutes. Serves 6.

Shrimp Creole

- 1/2 lemon, sliced
- 4 whole peppercorns
- 2 lbs shrimp, deveined

In a large pan bring 1 quart water to a boil, Add above ingredients; reduce heat and simmer for 3 minutes. Drain and reserve 1 cup liquid.

- 4 slices bacon, cup up
- 1 Tbls lemon juice
- 2 Tbls butter
- 1 tsp sugar
- 1 clove garlic
- 1 tsp salt
- 1 cup chopped onions
- 1/2 tsp salt
- 1 1/2 cups green pepper, chopped
- 1 Bay leaf
- 1 1/2 cup celery, sliced
- 1/4 tsp Tabasco
- 1 1 lb 12-oz. can tomatoes and juice
- 1/4 tsp thyme
- 1 6-oz. can tomato paste
- 3 cans water
- 1/4 tsp cayenne pepper
- 1/2 tsp filé powder

Sauté bacon in a dutch oven. Remove bacon from pan and add butter, garlic, onion, celery, and green pepper. Cook about 5 minutes. Add 1 cup reserved shrimp liquid, tomatoes, tomato paste, bacon, and lemon juice. Add tabasco, sugar, salt, pepper, bay leaf, and thyme. Bring to a boil, and simmer for 1 1/2 hours. Add shrimp and filé powder. Remove bay leaf before serving. This is a very good made the day before and refrigerated overnight.

Serve over rice.

Joey's Head and the Screen Door

LaRue is my aunt. She and I are close enough to the same age to be sisters. In fact, my mother, her sister, was 22 years old when LaRue was born and they were the only two children in the family. And, I might add for the new generation, they had the same parents.

LaRue's mother said to her one morning, "Honey, I wouldn't let Joe look after the baby if I were you." (Joe was the baby's daddy.) "Why not, Mother." "Well, he doesn't have good judgment." "Mother, why on earth would you say that?" To which my grandmother replied, "Honey, the other morning I saw him push the screen door open with the baby's head."

Isn't it amazing how children survive no matter what mistakes we make with them? And more than that, they love us anyway. I tried so hard not to make the same mistakes my parents made with me. And you know, it never occurred to me that I would make mistakes of my own.

My girls and I had somewhat of a gypsy life after their father and I divorced. My girls were three, five, and eight years old. I restored old houses for a living in Houston back in the late '70s, which meant we moved according to the capital gains laws: every six months, nine months or year. I made the remark one time when I came under criticism for moving my children so frequently, that, yes, we had moved a lot but I always had them in the same school. My middle daughter said, "Sure Mama, I'm in the seventh grade and I've been to eight schools." I was astonished as she reeled them off to me. But you know what? They're very flexible. And they even admit to getting a little antsy if they are in one house or town more than two years.

It seems every negative experience has a positive to it, if you look for it. My teenage life was disrupted by the progressive alcoholism of my mother. With that came increasing frustration and anger for my father which prompted violent temper outbursts. The unexpectedness of those clashes caused me to instantly withdraw and become very calm. This translated into my adult life as a cool head in crisis. That happened to be a highly valued trait for my job as a flight attendant and certainly was critical for the rearing of my three daughters alone. A child who survives an alcoholic home has great courage, some are super achievers — Babe Ruth's father was alcoholic and extremely abusive. Another strong trait of most children of alcoholic parents is a great sense of humor. It is developed in order to diffuse tense and sometimes dangerous situations.

The point of this is that most children love their parents no matter what. We can go a long way with them by asking for their forgiveness for the mistakes we know we have made with them as well as those we aren't aware of. We all did the best we could at the time. You can bet if we had known a better road we would have traveled it.

Be ye kind one to another, tenderhearted, forgiving one another, even as God for Christ's sake hath forgiven you. — **Ephesians 4:32**

Stuffed Snapper

- 2 cups cooked shrimp and crab meat
- 1 3 lb snapper
- 2 eggs
- 1 cup cream
- 2 Tbls butter
- 1/2 cup chopped mushrooms
- 2 tsp chopped chives
- 1 Tbls flour
- salt and paprika
- 4 Tbls Sherry
- 2 limes

Mix shrimp, eggs and 1/2 cup cream together. Melt butter, add to mushrooms and chives, sauté until soft. Add flour and cook until bubbly. Add crab meat mixture and stir until thick. Place fish in buttered baking dish. Stuff the fish with crab mixture. Pour over remaining cream and sprinkle with salt and paprika. Pour sherry over all. Bake 350 degrees 45 minutes. Serve with limes.

Tuna Casserole

- 1 can water packed tuna
- 1 can mushroom soup
- 1 soup can, 1/2 milk and 1/2 water
- 4 red potatoes
- 1 medium onion
- parsley
- 1 can fried onion rings

Butter casserole dish. Layer potatoes, tuna, sliced onions, chopped parsley and a soup spoon of mushroom soup, about 3 layers. You should have about 1/2 soup can left of soup, fill up the rest of the can with milk and stir. Pour on top of the tuna mixture. You may top with canned fried onion rings if desired. Bake at 350 degrees for about 45 minutes until potatoes are done.

Tamale Pie

- 2 Tbls butter
- 1 1/2 pounds ground beef
- 1 onion diced
- 1 clove minced garlic
- 2 cups canned tomatoes
- 1 6-oz. can tomato paste
- 1 14-oz. can drained corn, whole kernel Green Giant niblets
- 1 cup chopped celery
- 1 12-oz. package frozen lima beans
- 1 Tbls chili powder
- 2 tsp salt
- 1/4 tsp pepper
- 1 1/2 cups sifted all purpose flour
- 3 tsps baking powder
- 1 tsp salt
- 1 cup cornmeal
- 1/4 cup shortening
- 1 cup milk
- 1 egg yolk
- 1 Tbls cold water

Heat butter in large, heavy saucepan. Add ground beef and cook gently, stirring often until crumbly and lightly browned. Add onion and garlic and continue cooking and stirring 2 minutes more. Add tomatoes, tomato paste, corn, lima beans, celery, chili powder, salt and pepper. Cover and simmer 20 minutes, stirring occasionally. Remove from heat and let cool slightly while preparing dough. Heat oven to 375 degrees. Sift flour, baking powder, and salt into mixing bowl. Add cornmeal and stir lightly with a fork Add shortening and cut in coarsely. Add milk and stir lightly with a fork just until all dry ingredients are moistened, gather into a ball and knead lightly about 6 times on floured board. Use two thirds of dough and roll into a round large enough to line bottom and sides of a 2-quart casserole and extend a little over the edge. Pour meat filling into casserole when it is lined in this way. Roll remaining dough quite thin and cut into strips 1 inch wide. Lay these strips in lattice fashion on top of pie, letting strips extend over edge. Turn edge of bottom lining and end strips under and flute to make a high edge. Beat egg yolk and water together and brush on lattice. Bake at 375 degrees about 25 minutes or until pastry is well browned and filling is bubbly. Serves 8.

Salads

Mama's Dishwasher

My sister, Dannette, and I were laughing recently about how laid back our mother was in so many ways, as we both are too. That is if you can be high strung and laid back at the same time.

Mama had a dish washer. It wasn't her first but apparently it took Daddy several years to catch on to what was going on. Mama never emptied the dishwasher. She took clean dishes and silverware and glasses out to use and when the meal was over she put the dirty dishes in the dishwasher and ran a load. Apparently, one night it clicked with Daddy what she was doing and he threw a ring-tailed fit. Of all the carrying on he did about that being the stupidest thing he's ever seen, she was washing some of the dishes over again etc. etc. etc.

She just listened to him for a while and finally said, "Dan, what difference does it make?"

He was speechless.

Dannette and I just broke up over her simple logic. Next time you're getting your panties in a wad over something, stop and ask yourself, "What difference does it make?"

Now as they went on their way, he entered a village; and a woman named Martha received him into her house. And she had a sister called Mary, who sat at the Lord's feet and listened to his teaching. But Martha was distracted with much serving; and she went to him and said, "Lord, do you not care that my sister has left me to serve alone? Tell her then to help me." But the Lord answered her, "Martha, Martha, you are anxious and troubled about many things. One thing is needful. Mary has chosen the good portion, which shall not be taken away from her." — **Luke 10:38**

Asparagus Salad with Papaya Salsa

- 32 fresh asparagus spears
- 1/2 cup diced purple onion
- 2 Tbls chopped fresh chives
- 1 tsp minced fresh garlic
- 1/4 cup fresh lime juice
- 2 Tbls canola oil
- 1/2 tsp salt
- 1/8 tsp pepper
- 2 ripe papayas, peeled and chopped
- 1 lb romaine lettuce

Snap tough ends of asparagus; cook in microwave 4 minutes. Plunge into ice water to stop the cooking process; drain and set aside. Whisk together onion and next six ingredients in a medium bowl; add papaya, and gently toss. Arrange asparagus spears, lettuce leaves, and salsa evenly on individual serving plates. Makes 4 servings.

This is the best salad I've ever tasted and I'm not a fan of papaya.

Banana Dressing
(for fruit salad)

- 2 ripe bananas
- 2 Tbls lemon juice
- 1/4 cup brown sugar
- 1/4 cup honey
- 1 cup heavy cream whipped

Put bananas, juice, sugar and honey into blender. Process until smooth. Fold in whipped cream.

❦ Christine Griffin

Blueberry Congealed Salad

- 1 can blueberries
- 2 pkg concord grape Jello
- 1 medium can of crushed pineapple
- 1 1/2 cups of hot water
- topping (see below)

Mix all ingredients together and let set 1 hour in refrigerator or until congealed. Top with topping.

Topping
Soften 1 8-oz. pkg cream cheese at room temperature or microwave; then add 1/2 cup sour cream and 1/2 cup sugar or less to liking; add 1 teaspoon lemon juice and 1 teaspoon of vanilla flavoring; mix all together then top your dessert.

🍓 Marge Quimby

Egg Salad

For sandwiches

- 3 hardboiled eggs
- 2 Tbls mayonnaise
- 2 Tbls chopped olives or capers
- pepper

Hard boil eggs and mash with a potato masher. Add olives or capers and mayonnaise. Stir well. Do not add salt unless you taste first and think it needs it. Add pepper to taste.

Serve on whole wheat bread.

Great Sunday night supper: egg salad sandwiches and tomato soup.

Basil Vinaigrette

- 2/3 cup olive oil
- 2/3 cup white wine vinegar
- 1/4 cup finely chopped fresh basil
- 2 green onions, finely chopped
- 1 tsp salt
- 1/2 tsp pepper

Process all ingredients in a food processor or blender, stopping once to scrape down sides. Cover mixture, and chill. Stir well, and toss with mixed greens. Makes 1 1/3 cups.

Garlic Vinaigrette

- 4 garlic cloves
- 2 shallots
- 1/4 cup chopped fresh parsley
- 1/2 tsp dried crushed red pepper
- 1/2 tsp salt
- 1/2 tsp pepper
- 2 Tbls white wine vinegar
- 2/3 cup olive oil

Pulse garlic and shallots in a food processor 3 or 4 times. Add parsley and next 4 ingredients; process 20 seconds, stopping once to scrape down sides. Pour oil through food chute in a slow steady stream with processor turning; process mixture until blended. Makes 1 cup.

Dannette's Salad Dressing

- 3 Tbls lemon juice
- 1 clove garlic, minced or pressed
- 1/8 tsp salt (or to taste)
- 6 Tbls olive oil

Thoroughly mix together with fork. Serves 3.

❦ Dannette Brooks

Gazpacho Congealed Salad

- 1 7-oz. jar pimentos, drained
- 1 large cucumber, diced
- 1 green pepper, slivered
- 3 firm tomatoes, diced
- 4-5 green onions, chopped
- 1 cup pitted black olives, sliced
- 1 small clove garlic, mashed
- 2 Tbls olive oil
- 1 Tbls cider or wine vinegar
- salt and pepper to taste
- 1 can undiluted consomme
- 1 pkg apple flavored gelatin
- 1 envelope unflavored gelatin
- 3 cups boiling water
- 3 hard boiled eggs, quartered

Melt gelatin in boiling water until dissolved. Put in refrigerator and cool until thick. Mix vegetables together and let set an hour, then add to consomme mix. Pour into 2 1/2-3 quart mold and chill until firm. To serve, turn out on large plate garnish with eggs. Makes 8-10 servings.

For quick easy service, chill the salad mixture in an oiled shallow square or oblong pan; cut in squares to serve

Curry Dressing

- 1 cup mayonnaise
- 1/4 cup honey
- 1/4 cup red wine vinegar
- 2 tsps curry powder

Whisk all together all ingredients in a small bowl until blended. Cover and chill at least 1 hour. Serve over mixed salad greens. Makes 1 2/3 cups.

Cowboy Salad

- 1 can ranch style beans
- 1 cup grated cheese
- 1 tomato, peeled and cubed
- 1 small onion, sliced
- 2 cloves garlic, crushed
- 1 bottle Catalina dressing
- 1 head iceberg lettuce, shredded
- 1 medium bag original size corn chips

Drain beans and wash. Add cheese, tomato, onion, garlic and dressing. Marinate overnight in fridge. When ready to serve, add lettuce and corn chips and toss thoroughly.

Note: Do not put the chips or lettuce in too early. The lettuce will wilt and the chips will be soggy.

🍴 Ida Sing

Cranberry Salad

- 2 cups fresh cranberries
- 2 cups water
- 2 cups sugar
- 2 boxes lemon Jello
- 1 cup chopped pecans
- 1 medium can crushed pineapple

Boil cranberries in water until they pop. Take off the heat and add sugar and jello. Stir well and let cool, then add pecans and crushed pineapple. Refrigerate. Cut in squares and serve on crisp lettuce.

🍴 Marci Griffin

Lady from Hawaii and the Deaf Man

When I was a fairly new flight attendant we ran into some particularly dangerous weather over New Orleans. This was in the early 1960s when Delta, National and American Airlines had several trips that flew to and from the West and East Coast using the same piece of equipment. This was for the benefit of the passengers so that they were able to stay on one plane from coast to coast. The different airline crews were the ones that changed. American flew the plane from the West Coast to Dallas, Delta took it to New Orleans and then National crews flew it to Miami. On this particular day we had to overfly New Orleans and the Delta crew flew the aircraft on to Miami.

On the way back from Miami, the flight was worked by National crews and we were seated as regular passengers. (In the airline lingo this is called "dead-heading.")

The weather had cleared a little bit so we were able to land this time in New Orleans, and at this point the Delta crew resumed command.

I was greeting the passengers and checking tickets when I looked up to see a man carrying his invalid wife up the stairs. When they got to me she exclaimed, "Oh, Honey, this isn't anything like what we're used to, our weather is beautiful." I asked her where they were from and she said, "We live in Hawaii, dear." Time stood still.

I began to recall a TV program I had seen several months earlier. I said, "Did *Kraft Suspense Theater* do a program about you?" "Yes, Dear." I started crying and hugged her and her husband as well.

Her husband was an engineer and had been called to one of the outer islands. She was home alone. She was in a wheel chair and could live comfortably by herself but this was not an ordinary day. The weather had been fierce and suddenly the sirens started wailing alerting everyone that a tidal wave was imminent. She grabbed up the phone to call for help but it was already dead. She got to the front door and then lowered herself out of the wheelchair to negotiate the steps and began to drag herself to the white wooden gate, calling for help all the time. It was uncommonly quiet now because most of her neighbors had already left.

A salesman, new to the island, found himself lost in the suburbs. He had wandered around trying to get his bearings but to no avail. He couldn't hear the sirens wailing. He was deaf. He had no idea of the immediate peril he faced. He saw a small house surrounded by a white picket fence; something told him to stop there and ask for directions. He found my friend crumpled up by the gate unable to get it open to go any further. She was able to communicate to him the danger they faced and they escaped, saving each other's lives.

Psalms 91:11-12 — *For he will give his angels charge of you to guard you in all your ways. On their hands they will bear you up, lest you dash your foot against a stone.*

Roquefort Dressing

- 1 8-oz. package cream cheese, softened
- 1 8-oz. container sour cream
- 1 clove garlic, minced
- 1/4 cup half and half
- 3 Tbls white wine vinegar
- 1/4 tsp salt
- 1 4-oz. package crumbled blue cheese
- 4 oz. Roquefort cheese crumbled

Beat first six ingredients at medium speed with an electric mixer until blended. Stir in cheeses. Makes 4 cups.

Note: for thinner consistency, add additional half-and-half.

Seafood Salad and Fruit

- Alaskan King crab meat or fresh shrimp
- 1 bunch of asparagus spears
   Microwave on high for 2 1/2 minutes in a little water covered with cellophane, drop in ice water to halt cooking and then chill.
- 1 package fresh fruit, such as cantaloupe, honeydew and watermelon
- slices of fresh pineapple
- slices of papaya
- salad dressing over all

Salad Dressing
In a jar mix:
- 3 Tbls olive oil
- 1/4 cup wine vinegar
- 1 Tbls snipped cilantro
- 1 Tbls honey
- juice of one lemon or lime
- dash salt and pepper

Green Goddess Salad Dressing

- 1 clove garlic
- 6 anchovy fillets, cut up
- 2 Tbls minced chives
- 1 Tbls lemon juice
- 2 Tbls tarragon vinegar
- 2 Tbls sour cream
- 1 cup mayonaise
- 2 Tbls minced parsley
- salt and freshly ground pepper to taste

Mix all ingredients well, chill and serve over any greens you like.

Dressing for Green Salad

- 1 small clove garlic, pressed
- 1/4 tsp salt
- 2/3 cup salad oil
- 1/3 cup red wine vinegar or balsamic vinegar
- 1/4 tsp dry mustard
- freshly ground pepper and salt to taste
- 1 tsp Worscestershire sauce

Combine garlic with salt and a few drops of oil. Add salad oil, vinegar, mustard, pepper, and Worcestershire sauce. Beat with a rotary beater until mixture is well blended. Keep in covered jar in refrigerator until ready to use. Makes 1 cup.

Honey French Dressing

- 1/4 cup sugar
- 1 tsp dry mustard
- 1 tsp paprika
- 1 tsp celery seed
- 1/4 tsp salt
- 1/3 cup vinegar
- 1/2 cup honey
- 1 Tbls lemon juice
- 1/2 tsp grated onion

Mix above ingredients using electric beaters then add 1 cup salad oil very slowly all the while beating constantly.

🌹 Kay Harrison Barncord

Honey Yogurt Dressing

- 1 16-oz. carton vanilla yogurt
- 1/4 cup honey
- 3 Tbls lemon juice
- 1/4 tsp salt
- 1/8 tsp pepper

Combine yogurt and remaining ingredients; cover and chill. Makes 1 2/3 cups. Use on fruit salad.

West Indies Salad

- 1 lb can white lump crabmeat
- 1/2 onion finely chopped or sliced purple onion
- 1/3 cup olive oil
- juice of one lemon
- 4 Tbls ice water
- salt and pepper to taste

Mix all together and marinate at least 3 hours before serving.
Fresh ground pepper on top to taste.

Mama and the Tiger

My mother suffered from the disease of alcoholism. She was a periodic: she drank alcoholically for several days straight and then wouldn't touch a drop for two or three months.

One afternoon she dropped by to see my grandmother. Mama told her that she had had a most interesting experience that morning. She was driving down Ann St. and a big tiger ran across the road in front of her. My grandmother, in typical enabling fashion said, "Oh, is that right, dear? That must have scared you." But in her head she was saying to herself: "Poor Annette, she's getting worse. She's beginnning to hallucinate, she's seeing tigers in the middle of town now."

Later that night as Grandmother was watching the 10 o'clock news, the announcer said that the Ringling Bros. Barnum and Bailey Circus had a train mishap going through Montgomery and some of the animals had gotten loose. They had now recaptured them.

When we make a new discovery or become aware of a problem or a change we have entered the first phase of the three As: awareness, acceptance, and action. We become aware. Nothing can be done at all until we become aware that a problem exists. When we become aware this means our denial is starting to crumble. At this stage there is pain as we grasp this new truth. In our effort to avoid pain we often skip over acceptance and jump right into action. This is putting the cart before the horse. We must accept this new truth before we are able to decide what the appropriate action is. When I first became aware that I was an alcoholic (not just a problem drinker), the realization shocked me. But, fortunately for me, acceptance (or surrender) followed swiftly. I was tired of fighting this terminal something and I was ready to jump right into recovery (action). Many times a person has a vague notion of what is happening and when they see the pain looming ahead they jump into action before they've had time to accept and see the problem for what it is. When you jump into action before acceptance, often the action will be inappropriate or just won't stick. For example, if I had jumped into recovery before I really accepted that I had a bad problem with alcohol, I might not have stuck with the program. This often happens in AA. A person comes to eliminate the pain or to please the spouse and because he/she is not sure there really is a problem, he/she will return to the drinking behavior. So the second step is acceptance and then we move into action. At this point the problem has been thought through, all the alternatives weighed and then the appropriate action. This formula can be applied to most any problem one encounters.

"Acceptance does not mean submission to a degrading situation. It means accepting the fact of a situation, then deciding what we will do about it." (From *One Day at the Time* in Al-Anon). Acceptance makes choice possible.

When he, the Spirit of truth, is come, he will guide you into all truth. — **John 16:13**
Ye shall know the truth and the truth shall set you free. — **John 8:32**

Tomato Aspic

Melt Knox gelatin in medium sized V-8 juice in little sauce pan on stove.When the gelatin is melted, pour juice in Pyrex dish. Add:
* *chopped celery*
* *green or red pepper if desired*
* *green onions*
* *sliced avocado*
Put in refrigerator until set, probably 2 hours.

Slice in squares and place on a lettuce leaf. Top with dollop of mayonnaise or sour cream.

🌿 Annette Brooks

Cucumber Sauce for Aspic
* 1 cup mayonaise
* 1 cup chopped cucumber
* 2 Tbls chopped chives
* 1 tsp chopped parsley
* 1/2 tsp salt
* 1/2 tsp dill (dried or fresh)
Combine and mix well. Makes 1 1/2 cups

Patti's Cooked Relish

* 1 small can sliced mushrooms
* chopped green or red pepper
* chopped green chilis (in a can)
* 1 small jar pimentos

Cook all of this in a little butter. Add about 1 teaspoon cumin and 1 teaspoon curry powder. Serve on the side with chicken, or put a can of hominy in it and serve it over brown rice.

Lemon Poppy Seed Dressing

- 2 Tbls poppy seeds
- 1/4 cup honey
- 1/2 cup salad oil
- 1 tsp grated onion
- 3/4 tsp salt
- 1/3 cup freshly squeezed lemon juice

(Optional) Put poppy seeds in blender and blend on high speed until crushed about 1 minute.

Add honey, salad oil, cinnamon, coriander and salt. Blend until well mixed. Add lemon juice, onion juice, and blend until creamy. Store in a tightly covered jar in refrigerator until ready to use. Use on fruit salad or greens and fruit. Makes 1 cup.

Sauerkraut Salad

- 1 large can kraut, drained
- 1 cup thinly sliced or chopped green pepper
- 1 cup chopped celery
- 1 4-oz. can diced pimento
Mix together.

Add mixture of:
- 2/3 cup vinegar
- 1/3 cup water
- 1/2 cup salad oil
- 1 1/4 cup sugar

Marinate at least 2 hours. Serve cold.

❦ Sara Brooks

Thai Noodle Salad

- 6 oz vermicelli or thin spaghetti
- 1/4 cup reduced sodium soy sauce
- 1/2 cup chicken or vegetable broth
- 2 Tbls reduced fat peanut butter
- 1 Tbls fresh lime juice
- 1 tsp minced garlic
- 1 tsp minced ginger root or 1/2 tsp ground ginger
- 1/2 tsp crushed red pepper
- 3/4 lb boiled shrimp
- 1 red sweet pepper, cut into thin bite size pieces
- 3 green onions, cut diagonally into 1/2 inch pieces
- 1 can sliced or slivered water chestnuts
- 1/4 cup fresh cilantro
- lime wedges
- 2 Tbls finely chopped peanuts (optional)

Cook vermicelli according to package directions; drain. Combine soy sauce, broth, peanut butter, lime juice, garlic, ginger root, and crushed red pepper in a saucepan. Cook and stir over low heat until peanut butter is melted. Add cooked pasta; toss to coat. Add shrimp, red pepper, green onion and cilantro. Mix well. Serve warm or let stand at room temperature up to 1 hour. Serve with lime wedges. Garnish with peanuts if desired. Bakes 4 servings.

This is great, and so quick and easy.

Tomato, Red Onion, Pine Nuts and Mint Salad

Mint Oil
• 1 bunch fresh mint leaves
• 4 Tbls extra virgin olive oil

Pureé mint leaves in a blender with olive oil. Strain mixture through a cheesecloth into a small jar and reserve.

Vinaigrette
• 2 Tbls sherry vinegar
• 1 Tbls lemon juice
• 2 tsp minced shallots
• 1 clove garlic, peeled and minced
• 4 Tbls virgin olive oil
• salt and pepper to taste

Mix together the vinegar, lemon juice, shallots and garlic in a small bowl and let stand for 15 minutes. Slowly whisk in olive oil. Season with salt and pepper to taste. Set aside.

Salad
• 3 ripe tomatoes, thinly sliced
• 4 Tbls pine nuts, toasted
• 12 fresh mint leaves, finely chopped
• 8 fresh chives, chopped
• fresh mint springs for garnish

To serve, divide tomato slices among 4 plates. Scatter onions over tomatoes. Sprinkle with pine nuts, fresh mint and chives. Drizzle mint oil and vinaigrette on top. Garnish with fresh mint sprigs. Serves 4.

Pass a Little Time

Joe told me he had a problem. It was his secretary. She had written a scathing letter to him and called him abusive.

The scenario went like this. He is CEO of a corporation on the East Coast. She was there when he came on. Every morning she spoke to him when he arrived for work, but did not come to his office unless he summoned her for secretarial duties. Several times he came in after a long weekend or some vacation time and they exchanged the perfunctory "Good Morning." He asked her several times if she was interested in what he had done. Her reply was that his personal business was no concern of hers. Over the months he felt an anger building towards her and it was only after this incident that it became apparent.

The building help had been watering down the liquid soap in the bathrooms to conserve money. Joe had asked them not to do this but apparently his request had gone unheeded. The day it came to a head was when he was washing his hands in his executive bathroom and because the soap was so thin it splashed up on him and left a stream of soap suds all over his shirt, tie and pants. He walked down to where the employees were and said, "I have asked you not to water down the soap. I am now telling you. Don't water down the soap!" This with an edge of irritation to it. It was this scene that prompted the abuse letter.

I couldn't help but smile a little and said, "Joe, I know exactly what the problem is. It has to do with the morning greeting. We have a cultural difference here."

You see, Joe and I are from the Deep South. There is a certain discourse which has to be followed before the business at hand is discussed. It goes like this: "Good morning, Mr. Goodson, how are you? How is your wife? Where are your daughters now." He tells you all his personal news and then he says, "Patti, how's your Daddy? I haven't seen him in quite awhile. Has he been doing much fishing lately? How is your daughter doing at the university?" Etc., etc. Then, Mr. Goodson will take the lead because he is the president of the bank, and he will say, "What can I do for you today?" Whereupon I say, "Well, Mr. Goodson, I have a house I'd like to remodel and I need to borrow $5000." We will now discuss terms, etc. This is the order, first a bit of socializing then the object of the visit. If I had sat down and immediately said what was on my mind, "Mr. Goodson, I'd like to borrow $5000." He would say, "Patti, how's your daddy?" Etc., etc. You have to follow this line of pleasantries first or no business gets done.

Joe's secretary being from north of the Mason-Dixon line did not know about this. In fact, she had reiterated to him on several occasions that his personal business was his own. Although Joe was not aware of the dynamic here, he was slowly feeling more isolated and alone as time went on because no one was taking any personal interest in him. This was also leading to feelings of anger and frustration. So in our scenario here, the watered down soap was not the problem.

All Joe required was just a few minutes of inquiring about his weekend: "Joe, did you have a good time on your trip? What did you eat in Nassau? Were your accommodations good?" Three minutes chat on Monday morning could have saved three months of slow boil.

We live in a very impersonal world now. Let's remember to ask our waiter how he's doing, the bank teller how her grandchild is? Just a few words make our hearts warm, and make us feel that we belong.

John 14:34-35 — *A new commandment I give to you, that you love one another; even as I have loved you, that you also love one another. By this all men will know that you are my disciples, if you have love for one another.*

Sauces and Dressings

Patti and the Mixmaster

When I was a little girl I loved to watch my mother cook. One memorable day she was making banana pudding. She had layered the bowl with vanilla wafers, she had made the pudding part, and at this point was beating the egg whites for the meringue. I was sitting on the counter by the big old fashioned mix-master fascinated by this whole process. I would become mesmerized by the beaters and lean down towards the bowl. Mama would say, "Get back, Patti, you're getting too close." She continued beating and this conversation took place several times. I leaned over the last time, one time too many, when the beaters caught my shoulder length hair and in a flash my hair had been wound to the scalp, and my head was in the bowl with the beaters still grinding away. Of course, I was screaming bloody murder; my mother had fallen back against the counter laughing hysterically unable to do anything. Fortunately for me, my grandmother heard the racket and ran into the kitchen where the mix-master and I were now rolling around in the middle of the kitchen floor and unplugged the monster machine. I spent the rest of second grade with my hair parted on the other side to cover the bald spot.

Twenty-five years later I was in the kitchen making a pound cake with my two youngest little daughters sitting on the counter watching me. They started hugging each other and I had no sooner gotten it out of my mouth to be careful when out of the corner of my eye, in slow motion, they tumbled head over heels off the counter top and landed in a pile at my feet. I fell back against the counter in absolute laughing convulsions. They both lay there for a few moments, not knowing whether to laugh or cry and then they both broke out in laughter, no harm done.

We all have choice about how we react to events. My mother taught me a very good lesson in the drama I described above. There wasn't going to be any "Poor pitiful Patti" with her big bald spot. Instead, she very practically changed the part in my hair, covering the spot, and assured me my hair would grow back in. No victim here.

My own children might have been a little banged up and momentarily frightened, but they each chose to make it a comic event. Always remember this. You *can* change your reaction to things. In fact, the correct word here is, choose to *respond* rather than *react*. One means take a few moments to think. The other means don't think, just act.

And be not conformed to this world: but be ye transformed by the renewing of your mind, that ye may prove what is that is good, and acceptable, and perfect, will of God. — **Romans 12:2**

Dipping Sauce for Meat (Chicken Fingers)

- 1/2 cup mayonnaise
- 1/4 cup olive oil
- 3 Tbls chile sauce
- 2 Tbls catsup
- 1 Tbls water
- 2 tsp Worcestershire sauce
- 2 tsp yellow mustard
- 1 tsp coarsely ground black pepper
- dash of paprika
- dash of Tabasco
- 1 small onion minced
- 1 clove garlic, minced

Combine all ingredients; cover and chill. Makes 2 cups.

Ham Glaze

- 1/2 cup French's mustard, any flavor
- 1/2 cup orange marmalade *
- 1/2 tsp ground ginger

Combine ingredients. Brush mixture on ham frequently during the last hour of baking. Makes one cup (enough for 10-15 lb ham).

* May substitute 1/2 cup brown sugar for marmalade.

Jalapeño Sauce

- 3/4 cup plain nonfat yogurt
- 1 clove garlic, minced
- 1/4 cup seeded and chopped jalapeño peppers
- 1/4 cup chopped fresh cilantro
- 1 tsp frozen unsweetened orange juice concentrate, thawed
- 1/2 tsp ground cumin
- 1/4 tsp salt

Combine all ingredients. Makes 1 cup.

Bechamel Sauce

In a heavy saucepan, heat 1 tablespoon of olive oil over medium heat. Add 1 1/2 tablespoons all purpose flour and cook, stirring constantly for 2-3 minutes, until the flour begins to turn golden. Gradually pour in 2 cups low-fat milk. Cook, stirring constantly, until the mixture comes to a simmer. Season with salt, pepper and nutmeg to taste.

Remoulade Sauce

- 8 Tbls mayonnaise
- 3 Tbls horseradish mustard
- 1 Tbls vinegar, white
- 2 Tbls olive oil
- 1/2 clove minced garlic and equal amount minced onion

Mix all together and add a few drops Tabasco and some black pepper. Chill.

Serve with boiled shrimp.

Rosemary-Red wine Vinegar

- 7 6-inch fresh rosemary sprigs
- 4 cups red wine vinegar

Place rosemary sprigs in a 1 quart jar. Bring red wine vinegar to a boil. Pour over rosemary in jar. Cover and let stand at room temp 2 days. Remove and discard rosemary; chill vinegar up to 6 months. Makes 3 -3/ 4 cups.

White Sauce

Make a sauce of 3 tablespoons of flour sifted in 4 tablespoons of oil, cook on low heat and stir constantly. When mixed, add two cups of milk, stirring all the time. Salt and pepper to taste.

"First you make a Roux"

- 1/4 cup butter or oil
- 1/4 cup flour

Melt oil and blend flour, stirring constantly until mixture is light brown. If possible cook this in an iron skillet.

Tomato Basil Sauce

- 1 small onion, chopped
- 4 cloves garlic, chopped
- 2 Tbls olive oil
- 1 cup dry red wine
- 1/2 tsp salt
- 1/4 tsp freshly ground pepper
- 2 28-oz. cans diced tomatoes
- 1/2 cup fresh basil leaves, shredded

Sauté chopped onion and garlic in hot oil in a large saucepan until tender. Add dry red wine, salt, and pepper, and cook, stirring occasionally, 5 minutes. Add diced tomatoes; reduce heat, and simmer, stirring often, 30 minutes. Cool mixture slightly. Process half of tomato mixture in a blender or food processor until smooth, stirring once to scrape down sides; return to saucepan. Repeat procedure with remaining tomato mixture. Cook over medium heat until sauce is throughly heated, and stir in shredded basil. Serve over favorite pasta. Makes 5 cups.

Vegetarian Tomato Sauce

- 1/2 med onion, coarsely chopped
- 2 cloves garlic,coarsely chopped
- 1 tsp dried oregano
      Double the herb amounts for fresh herbs.
- 1 tsp dried basil
- 1/2 cup chopped green pepper
- 1 cup quartered button mushrooms

Heat 1 teaspoon of extra-light olive oil mixed with a dash of toasted sesame oil in a saucepan over medium heat and sauté 1/2 onion, garlic, basil and oregano until the onion starts to turn transparent about 5 minutes. Add green pepper and mushrooms, cover and cook 5 minutes. Pour in one 28-oz can of crushed tomatoes and their juice, bring to a boil, reduce the heat and simmer for 5 minutes.

Serve immediately over your favorite pasta. Serves 4.

Al's Tomato Gravy

- bacon
- 1 medium onion finely chopped
- canned tomatoes or fresh tomatoes
- Tabasco sauce

Fry three slices of bacon. Remove form the pan and let drain. Brown the onions in the bacon grease. Add the tomatoes and crumbled bacon. Tabasco to taste and a little olive oil for flavor.

Serve on biscuits or toast points. Can be served directly on eggs.

Dannette's Tomato Gravy

- 1 Tbls bacon grease
- 1 cup milk
- 2-3 fresh tomatoes
- 1 Tbls flour

Sauté one medium onion and 2-3 fresh tomatoes, all chopped. Stir in 1 Tablespoon of flour. Salt and pepper to taste. Add 1 cup of milk slowly, stirring all the while.

Serve over homemade biscuits.

Tip Your Hat and Say, Yes, M'am

A young friend of mine was sharing with me the other day about a situation she was in. She told me she was dating a man who was getting a divorce and she was at his house. His teen-age daughter came over unannounced. He opened the door, greeted her and then walked out on the porch with her and talked to her a little bit. She, sensing that she was intruding, decided to push the issue and walked into the house. My friend felt extremely awkward but her date did not offer to introduce them. The young lady walked on through the house and, making a big display of her displeasure, finally left. My friend had gotten upset with her date by this time so she left shortly after. She told me she was totally at a loss as to how to have better handled an awkward situation for all.

Many of us have grown up in dysfunctional families. We are totally thrown for a loop on occasions and do not know how to respond to situations because we didn't have good role models to follow. Instead of just backing up and punting, good manners are always appropriate. My friend could have offered her hand to the young lady and introduced herself. After all, she had done nothing wrong; she was an invited guest.

Good manners are to make people comfortable. When you find yourself not quite knowing how to deal with what's happening at a given time, fall back on plain old fashioned good manners to pull you through. It might not make the occasion pleasant but you will have gotten through an awkward moment with the satisfaction that you at least did the right thing.

Matthew 7:12 — *So whatever you wish that men would do to you, do so to them; for this is the law and the prophets.*

Soups

Uncle Charles and the Fish

My Uncle Charles was quite a character in the family. He owned a jewelry store and operated a loan company in Andalusia, Alabama, about 70 miles from Montgomery which is the state capital. When the legislature was in session, Uncle Charles would come to Montgomery, stay with us, and politic around up at the capitol. On one of his trips he brought up a mess of fresh bass and trout frozen and stored in half-gallon milk containers. He went by the office of the Speaker of the House and dropped some fresh fish off there, then went to the Senate chamber and left some there for some of his cronies, and then he went to the governor's mansion and left some there so Geroge Wallace could have some fresh caught fish.

Several weeks later, Aunt Inez was rummaging around in the freezer and called out to Uncle Charles if he knew where all those half-gallon milk containers had gone. He told her had taken them to Montgomery on his last trip up. It took all the control she had to keep from beating him half to death with the broom. "Charles, I've been saving chicken parts for months to go crabbing with and you've passed them out to every high office in the state."

You've heard it said that the road to hell is paved with good intentions. Not true. The road to *heaven* is paved with good intentions. In his book, *Seat of the Soul,* Gary Zukav says, "Intentions set into motion processes that affect every aspect of your life. If you desire to change your job, for example, that change begins with the intention to change." It is intention that we act on. We can think something with our heads but until it moves to our hearts with intention it will never happen.

For as he thinketh in his heart, so is he. — **Proverbs 23:7**

Brunswick Stew

- 2 2-1/2 lb whole chickens
- 2 qts water
- 1 Tbls salt
- 1 1/2 cups catsup, divided
- 2 Tbls light brown sugar
- 1 1/2 tsp dry mustard
- 1 1/2 tsp grated fresh ginger
- 1/2 lemon, sliced
- 1 garlic clove, minced
- 1Tbls butter
- 1/4 cup white vinegar
- 3 Tbls vegetable oil
- 1 Tbls Worcestershire sauce
- 3/4 tsp hot sauce
- 1/2 tsp pepper
- 2 28-oz. cans diced tomatoes
- 2 15 1/4-oz. cans whole kernel corn,undrained
- 2 14 3/4-oz. cans cream style corn
- 1 large onion, chopped
- 1/4 cup firmly packed light brown sugar
- 1 Tbls salt
- 1 Tbls pepper

Bring first three ingredients to a boil in a large heavy stock pot; cover, reduce heat, and simmer 45 minutes or until chicken is tender. Drain chicken, reserve 1 quart of broth in pot. Skin, bone, and shred chicken, and return to pot. Cook 1/2 cup catsup and next 11 ingredients in a small saucepan over medium heat, stirring occasionally, 10 minutes. Stir catsup mixture, remaining 1 cup catsup, tomatoes, and next six ingredients into chicken and broth; simmer, stirring often, 4 hours or until thickened. Makes 3 1/2 quarts.

Brunswick Stew is the Georgia version of Camp Stew.

Mrs. Mullins Camp Stew

Takes 2 days to prepare and several soup kettles.

- 6-7 lb hen (save stock)
- 6 lb pork shoulder (save stock)
- 3 lbs boneless beef stew (save stock)
- 3 lbs Irish potatoes, creamed
- 3 cans tomatoes
- 2 packages frozen green lima beans
- 3 cans cream style corn
- A-1 sauce and Worcestershire sauce
      I'm guessing:1 small bottle A-1 and Worcestershire
- red pepper and salt to taste

Cook meat until it comes form bone and mix in large vessel with all above ingredients; add the creamed potatoes along with the stock from meat and stir constantly.

☛ *Note from my mother: "The above takes hours to cook. After mixing, simmer for an hour or longer. My uneducated guess it will serve 10 people at least.*
☛ *Note: Mrs Mullins says in letter: "cook all day."*

This is great to cook ahead and store in freezer bags. You traditionally eat this with plain white bread. It's an accompaniment to barbecue.

Mrs. Mullins Barbeque Sauce
This sauce is mixed with cooked shredded chicken. It's like a hash.
- 1 cup water
- 1 cup vinegar
- 2 Tbls salt
- 1 cup butter or margerine
- red pepper and black pepper to taste
      Use lots.

Add some A-1 sauce if you like. Add a little sugar to taste, cook it real low and thick. Pour over chicken hash and mix thoroughly.

Mrs. Mullins is Aunt Katherine Brooks' mother. Aunt Katherine was married to Joe Brooks, my Daddy's youngest brother.

French Onion Soup

- 4-5 med sized onions
- 4 Tbls butter
- 1 Tbls flour
- 3 cans condensed beef broth
- 2 soup cans water
- 1 Tbls Worcestershire sauce
- 1/4 tsp pepper
- 8 slices French bread, 1 1/2 inches thick, cut from center of loaf
- 1/4 cup Parmesan cheese, grated
- 8 slices Swiss cheese

Peel and thinly slice onions. In a large saucepan, melt butter, add onions; slowly cook over med-low heat, stirring together, until onions are soft and golden brown, about 25 minutes. Sprinkle onions with flour. Cook for 1 minute, stirring constantly. Stir in broth, water, Worcestershire and pepper; bring to a boil. Reduce heat, cover; simmer 20 minutes.

While soup simmers, toast French bread slices under broiler or in a toaster oven.

Stir Parmesan cheese into soup, then ladle soup into individual ovenproof crocks, or pour it into a large ovenproof saucepan or soup tureen. Add toasted French bread slices to soup and top with slices of Swiss cheese. Place under broiler or bake in a 400-degree oven for 5 to 8 minutes until cheese has just melted and bubbles. Serves 4 to 6.

7-Day Detoxification Diet

To Prepare For Diet
☛ Twenty-four hours before starting, take a vegetable laxative. Repeat three or four days through the week.

☛ Take a warm bath every night. The first night, take an Epsom salts bath (one pound of salts to half a tub of water). This is extremely relaxing, but can also be very drying to the skin. As an alternative, use apple cider vinegar in the water.

☛ During the seven days, you will *not* eat:
• starches (no bread, cereal, rice, potatoes)
• proteins (no meat, fish, eggs, cheese, milk, nuts)
• sugars (raisins, dates, figs)
• fats (butter, cream, oils)
But you *will* eat as much and as often as you like:
• fresh fruits, except bananas
• green and fresh vegetables, cooked and served with lemon juice (no butter or sauces)
• clear broth made from the recipe below

First Day
Morning
• juice of one lemon in a glass of filtered or bottled water
• 15 to 30 minutes later, large glass of unsweetened grapefruit juice
10:30 A.M.
• 1 whole orange
Noon
• vegetable broth
• large lettuce and tomato salad dressed with lemon juice
3:00 P.M.
• glass of tomato juice
Dinner
• vegetable broth
• plate of cooked vegetables, such as carrots, spinach, cabbage
• salad of grated carrots and cubed celery, lemon juice dressing.
On Retiring
• 1 or 2 small apples or hot grapefruit juice.

Second Day
Morning
• juice of one lemon in filtered or bottled water
• half or whole grapefruit
Mid-morning
• large glass of tomato juice
Lunch
• vegetable broth
• large salad of shredded cabbage and pineapple (eat as much of this as you can chew thoroughly)
• 1 cooked vegetable, if desired
Mid-afternoon
• 1 or 2 apples or any fresh fruit, except bananas
Dinner
• vegetable broth
• plate of 3 cooked vegetables, such as beets, asparagus, onions, carrots
• salad of mixed vegetables
Desert
• berries or fresh pineapple

Third Day
Morning
• lemon juice in filtered or bottled water
• 2 large sliced oranges or one small grapefruit
Mid-morning
• tomato juice or 1 cup of fresh cherries or large serving of fresh or frozen fruit
Lunch
• vegetable broth
• large combination salad, lemon juice dressing
• 1 cooked vegetable, fresh fruit if desired
Mid-afternoon
• 1 cantaloupe or 1 grapefruit
Dinner
• vegetable broth
• tomato stuffed with cucumbers, celery, and finely chopped onions
• plate of cooked vegetables, such as diced white turnips, young beet greens, green peas

• fresh or frozen berries or cantaloupe for dessert
Before Retiring
• vegetable broth or tomato juice

Fourth Day
Morning
• lemon in filtered or bottled water on arising
• large dish of berries, cantaloupe or grapefruit, half-hour later
Mid-morning
• large glass of orange juice, whole orange is better
Lunch
• vegetable broth
• plate of chopped vegetables, such as beets, cauliflower, spinach with lemon dressing
• large fruit salad
Dinner
• vegetable broth
• large chef's salad, minus meat and cheese
• fruit salad or whole cantaloupe
On Retiring
• vegetable broth or tomato juice

The Fifth, Sixth, and Seventh Days
Continue as above. Repeat any day's menu or vary them with the same type of food at will.
☛ Note: On the 5th, 6th, and 7th days you may have honey with your fruit, if desired.
Morning
• grapefruit or orange, whole fruit of juice
Mid-afternoon
• tomato or fresh fruits
Dinner
• vegetable broth
• large salad
• 2 or 3 cooked vegetables
• fresh fruit for desert (cantaloupe and watermelon are satisfying and you may eat as much as you like of either)

Broth
- 1 bunch celery
- 1 bunch carrots
- 1 bunch parsley
- 1 lb greens

Cut up, place in large container, cover with water and boil gently. Remove all vegetables and add 2 quarts tomato juice and 1/2 cup Braggs Liquid Aminos.

You will not be hungry on this diet. Seven days will pass very quickly and the results you will get will be well worth the effort. You will feel so good. Your skin will clear up. You will be thrilled with the weight loss.

This diet is great for after holidays and vacations, times when it is easy to indulge in rich, heavy food. Lose what weight you may have gained.

Who's Going to Look After Whom?

Maureene and I have been best friends for years now. We each have three grown children and everybody is on their own and doing very well, thank you. We are both very even tempered and right laid back. We have felt a need lately to cover some issues that we consider quite important for that day in the future should it ever present itself. If, for some reason, in our old age, our kids decide to relinquish responsibility for us and place us in a retirement home, we are to keep an eye on each other. Our most important issue is that we make sure the other is not growing hairs where Southern ladies should not have them: namely, on our chins.

The other pact we have made with each other is that each of us is free to check the other's bathroom supplies and if, God forbid, we find jet black hair dye, it is to be whisked off the premises in a New York minute. After all, you see we are both former Delta Airlines flight attendants. Maureene is a former Miss Albany and runner-up in the Miss Georgia pageant, and I was in the Miss Loan and Pawn contest in Montgomery, Alabama, in 1957.

Recently, I had gone to see Maureene in Kansas City while she was in the seminary. I drove from Central Texas and the trip had been a long and arduous 13 hours. Being really tired from the long drive, I suggested to Maureene that we just have oatmeal that night. "I'll cook it because I have a secret for making it." I got the oatmeal started and when Maureene came in the kitchen I was busily hunting for the lid to the oatmeal box. She walked over lifted the lid of the pot looked at the gruel and closed it up again. Just about time for us to eat I said, "Maureene, I've looked everywhere including the garbage can for the oatmeal lid and I can't find it anywhere." She doubled up with laughter. "The lid is in the oatmeal. I saw it in there awhile ago when I looked at it. I thought that was your cooking secret." We both convulsed with laughter.

Now I ask you, who is going to look after whom when we're old and addled if we're doing this in our 50s?

Matt. 6:31-33 — *O Men of little faith. Therefore do not be anxious, saying, 'What shall we eat?' or ' What shall we drink?' or 'What shall we wear?' For the Gentiles seek all these things; and your heavenly Father knows that you need them all. But seek first his kingdom and his righteousness, and all these things shall be yours as well. Therefore do not be anxious about tomorrow, for tomorrow will be anxious for itself. Let the day's own trouble be sufficient for the day.*

Basic Fat Burning Soup

- 6 large green onions
- 1 or 2 cans (28 oz.) tomatoes
- 1 bunch celery
- 1 large cabbage
- 2 pkgs Lipton soup
- 2 cans water
- Season with salt, pepper, curry, parsley or hot sauce

Cut vegetables in small to medium pieces and cover with water. Boil fast for 10 minutes. Reduce to simmer and continue cooking until vegetables are tender. This soup can be eaten at any time you are hungry. Eat as much as you want, whenever you want. This soup will not add calories. The more you eat, the more you will lose.

☛ *Note: If eaten alone for indefinite period you will suffer malnutrition.*

Day One
All fruits except bananas. Cantaloupe and watermelon are lower in calories than most fruits. Eat only the fruits and soup. For drinks, unsweetened tea, cranberry juice or water.

Day Two
All vegetables, eat until your are stuffed with all the fresh raw or canned vegetables. Try to eat green leafy veggies and stay away from dry beans, peas and corn, eat along with the soup. At dinner time reward yourself with a baked potato and butter. Do not eat any fruits.

Day Three
Eat all the soup, fruits and vegetables you want. Do not have a baked potato. If you have eaten for three days as above and have not cheated, you will find that you have lost 5 to 7 pounds.

Day Four
Bananas and skim milk. Eat a many as three bananas and drink as many glasses of water as you can on this day along with the soup. Bananas are high in calories and carbohydrates and so is milk, but on this particular day your body will need the potassium and the carbohydrates, protein and calcium to lesson your craving for sweets.

Day Five
Beef and tomatoes. You may have as much as 10-20 oz of beef and a cup of tomatoes or 6 fresh tomatoes on this day. Try to drink at least 6-8 glasses of water this day to wash away the uric acid in your body. Eat the soup at least once today.

Day Six
Beef and vegetables. Eat to your hearts content all the beef and vegetables on this day. You can even have two or three steaks if you like, with green leafy vegetables, but no baked potato. Be sure to eat the soup at least once today.

Day Seven
Brown rice, unsweetened fruit juice and vegetables. Again stuff yourself. Be sure to have the soup at least once today.

The end of the seven day eating plan can be used as often as you like. As a matter of fact if correctly followed, it will clean you system of impurities and give you a feeling of well being as never before.

After only seven days of the process, you will begin to feel lighter by a least 10-17 pounds, having an abundance of energy. Continue this plan as long as you wish and feel the difference.

This diet is fast, fat-burning, and the secret is that you will burn more calories than you take in. It will flush your system of impurities and give you a feeling of well being. This diet does not lend itself to drinking any alcohol beverages at any time because of the removal of the fat buildup in your system. Go off the diet at least 24 hours before any intake of alcohol.

Because everybody's digestive system is different, this diet will affect everyone differently. After day three, you will have more energy than when you began, if you did not cheat. After being on this diet for several days, if you find your bowel movements have changed, eat a cup of bran or fiber. Although you can have black coffee with this diet you may find that you don't need the caffeine after the third day.

Definite No-Nos:
Bread, alcohol, carbonated drinks including diet drinks. Stick with water,

unsweetened tea, black coffee, unsweetened fruit juices, cranberry juice and skimmed milk.

The basic Fat Burning Soup can be eaten anytime you feel hungry. Eat as much as you wish. Remember the more you eat, the more you will lose. You can eat broiled or baked chicken instead of meat (absolutely no skin on the chicken).

Any prescribed medications will not hurt you on this diet. Continue this plan as long as you wish and feel the difference both mentally and physically. If you prefer, you can substitute broiled fish for the beef on only one of the beef days. You need high protein in the beef the other days.

❦ The Sacred Heart Memorial Hospital
Used for overweight heart patients to lose rapidly, usually before surgery.

U-Haul to West Texas

Back in 1982, I moved from Houston to Odessa. For those of you who don't know, Odessa is in West Texas and kind of hard to get to. My husband took a rather off-beat route that went along country roads until we finally got to some good highways. I was driving my car and he was pulling one of those large U-Haul trailers that virtually blocked his car from our view. As we drove through Austin there was a horrendous thunderstorm taking place. He never got below 60 miles per hour. I blew the horn at him, blinked my lights, everything I could think of to get his attention to slow down but to no avail. I had no choice but to follow his tail lights and pray. Finally we stopped for dinner and I got out of the car fussing. "I tried everything to get you to slow down. Please keep an eye on me behind you." His reply in his West Texas accent, "Well, Patti, I was thinking to myself these girls from Alabama sure know how to drive a car." He then got his two-bits in and told me to follow closer to him.

We left about dusk, finally picking up Interstate 10. I was following James but since there was no traffic to speak of I surely didn't feel like I needed to tailgate him, so my daughter and I talked and we let more distance get between us than I had realized. I sped up and finally got behind him at a more reasonable distance. It started to mist a little bit and we noticed that James would slow down, then speed up. We followed. I thought the U-Haul must be slipping on the damp pavement. This slowing down and speeding up went on until dark. Finally, the big U-Haul pulled over to the side of the interstate and I whipped right in behind. The headlights were still on, and as James got out of the car and started towards us, I noticed he had on a baseball cap I hadn't seen before. A few feet closer, I noticed his shirt was pulled out, and I had never known James to look that untidy. I rolled the car window down to see what he wanted when Dannette and I both gasped. The man said in a very loud voice, "Lady, why are you following me?" I started to mumble something while I was trying to get the window up and the doors locked when he said, "Your husband passed me about 45 minutes ago." I'm here to tell you that if that man had gone down one of those ranch house dirt roads I would have been right on his bumper until we got where he was going. Dannette, in distress, asked what we were going to do, and I said we were going to try to catch up with him but if we got to Sonora and had not located him I was going into a police station and turn ourselves in. James was pulled over on the side of the road about 15 minutes ahead of us, pacing. My other daughter, Claire, was in his car crying, thinking she would never see her mama and sister again.

We each have a guidance system that is unique to us. We must follow that guidance to get where God wants us to go in order to fulfill his purpose for us. Often, if we turn the guiding over to another human being, we end up following the wrong signs. We should never tell another person what he or she should do with their lives anymore than somebody can tell us. Follow your own guidance; sometimes the path might get a little foggy or slippery but stay quiet and listen to God speaking to you in His still small voice.

The kingdom of God is within you. — **Luke 17:21**

In quietness and in confidence shall be your strength. — **Isaiah 30:15**

New England Clam Chowder

- 5 large potatoes
- 2 sliced onions
- 2 chicken bouillon cubes
- 4 cups water
- 1 small can evaporated milk
- 1 can minced clams and juice

Cook until potatoes are about to fall apart. Drain off at least 2 cups of broth. Mash everything left in the pot with a potato masher. Add 1 small can of evaporated milk. Add one can of clams and juice along with the evaporated milk and heat through. Stir well.

Serve with French bread and butter. Put a good sprinkle of Tabasco on top when served.

Tuna Chowder

- 2 Tbls butter
- 1 small onion,chopped
- 1 can tuna, water packed
- 2 Tbls parlsey
- 1 can Campbell's potato soup

Melt the butter, add finely chopped onion and cook until just about transparent. Add tuna and parlsey and heat through. Add the potato soup and soup can with 1/2 water and 1/2 milk. Heat through. Serves 2.

Patti's Homemade Vegetable Soup

- 1 ham bone, or beef soup bone
- 1 onion, diced
- 2 cloves garlic, pressed
- 1/2 pt water
- 1/2 package frozen whole baby okra
- 1 can stewed tomatoes
- 1/2 cup pearl barley, rinsed until water is clear
- salt and pepper, 1 tsp of each
- any left over vegetables in fridge or
- 2 potatoes, cut in cubes
- 2 carrots, scraped and cut cross-wise
- can or pkg frozen baby green lima beans
- one small can mixed vegetables

Put 2 tablespoons of butter and 2 tablespoons olive oil in bottom of soup kettle. Heat and then lightly brown onions and garlic. Add tomatoes and bring to a boil. Taste for salt and pepper. (This first step is the secret of full bodied soup flavor.)

Add water, soup bone, okra, tomatoes , barley and salt and pepper. Reduce heat and simmer about an hour. Add remaining vegetables and simmer another 30 minutes. Serve with corn bread.

Potato Soup

- 5 large potatoes
- 2 sliced onions
- 2 chicken bouillon cubes
- 4 cups water

Cook until potatoes are about to fall apart. Drain off at least 2 cups of broth. Mash everything left in the pot with a potato masher. Add 1 small can of evaporated milk. Stir well. Serve with French bread and butter. Put a good sprinkle of Tabasco on top when served.

Variation
Add one can of clams and juice along with the evaporated milk and heat through.

Patti's Lamb-Barley Soup

• lamb bones, from leftover leg of lamb, or leg bones from grocery
• 1 1/2 qts water
• 1 can stewed tomatoes
• 3/4 cup pearl barley, washed until water is no longer cloudy
• 1 tsp salt
• 1 tsp black pepper
• carrots
• 1 can lima beans or half pkg frozen green baby limas
• left over wild rice or Uncle Ben's wild rice mix
• any leftover vegetables in refrigerator

Add water, lamb-bones, and barley and bring to a boil. Add salt and pepper and reduce heat and simmer about an hour. Add rice, limas, carrots, and any chopped vegetables, simmer for another 30 minutes. Serve with corn bread or some nice bakery bread with butter.

Patti's Southern Style Minestrone

- 1 ham bone with some ham on it
- 1 onion, diced
- 2 cloves garlic, pressed
- 1 can tomatoes
- 1 rutabaga
- 1/2 cup barley, washed until water runs clear
- 1 tsp each salt and pepper
- 1 can turnip greens
- 1 can navy beans
- 1/2 head of cabbage, sliced into 1/2-inch strips
- about dime size circumference of vermicelli or spaghetti

Put 2 tablespoons of butter and 2 tablespoons of olive oil in bottom of soup kettle. Heat and then lightly brown onions and garlic. Add tomatoes and bring to a boil. Taste for salt and pepper. (This first step is the secret of full bodied soup flavor.)

Bring ham bone, tomatoes, rutabaga and barley to a boil. Add salt and pepper and reduce heat and simmer about an hour. Add turnip greens, navy beans and cook about 20 minutes. Break spaghetti into 2 inch lengths and add to the soup, stirring well to keep it from lumping. About 10 minutes before serving, add the cabbage and stir it in. Let it wilt and then serve with corn bread.

Vegetables

You're Never Too Old

My handwriting has been so bad for so many years that I have considered it a handicap (like dyslexia of the handwriting). What happened as a result of this was an inability to communicate with the written word. I didn't write letters because no one could read them, and over time I lost my writing skills. When I went to the seminary this was a real challenge. We had lots of papers to write and I was totally dependent on the person who typed my papers. Since I couldn't write the original in long hand I had to have someone who could take dictation. You can see what a major issue this became.

I decided, albeit late, that I would not go into the next century much less next millennium computer illiterate. Mind you, I was one of those who came out of the 1950s reared to be "mistress of the manor" so I never even learned to type. I did take a typing course in 1984, and finished the class typing 26 words a minute with 28 errors.

At any rate, I bought a Macintosh computer in January 1994. I am not ashamed to tell you that I cried for the first month. I couldn't make the thing do anything I wanted it to. I finally took a day-long computer class in late February and I came away knowing two things about the computer: I couldn't tear it up and I was smarter than it was!

Those two pieces of knowledge removed the fear I associated with any kind of machinery. I began to learn a little more each day and I became willing to experiment a little with it. I don't know of anything that has given me as much pleasure in my adult life as this machine. The thrill of learning something this new has been exhilarating.

When we quit learning, we begin to get old no matter what our age. I hope I never lose the spark that makes me want to try new things. There are some old ones I don't have to do any more... like water-ski. I never liked it. I didn't like the speed. I didn't like falling and hurting myself. I'm old enough not to have to prove anything to anybody.

But I do like to challenge myself and prove to *me* that I can still learn new skills. I have now found that I have a wealth of family stories waiting to be saved by writing them down. My computer has become a real friend.

The Father that dwelleth in me, he doeth the works.
I am in the Father, and the Father in me. — **John 14:10-11**

Acorn Squash

About the size of your fist. If much larger they are almost impossible to cut in half.
• 1 tsp butter
• 1 Tbls brown sugar or honey
• cinnamon-sprinkle

Slice squash in halves. Place squash in Pyrex dish with about 1/2 inch water. Put pat of butter and teaspoon of brown sugar or honey in middle, sprinkle with cinnamon. Bake in microwave about 15 minutes.

Asparagus with Dill Sauce

• 1 cup mayonnaise
• 1 8-oz. container sour cream
• 1 Tbls minced onion
• 1 tsp dried dill
• 3 Tbls lemon juice
• 2 lbs asparagus
• 2 tbls lemon juice

Combine first five ingredients; cover and chill. Snap tough ends from asparagus. Arrange asparagus in a steamer basket over boiling water; cover and steam 4-5 minutes or until crisp-tender.

Variation
Cook asparagus in small amount of water in microwave (cover with plastic wrap) for about 3 minutes. Douse in ice water to stop cooking.

Arrange asparagus on a serving platter. Drizzle with 2 tablespoons of lemon juice. Serve with sauce. Makes 25 servings.

Black Beans Caribbean

- 1 lb package black beans
- 1 large onion, chopped medium fine
- 2 pods pressed garlic
- 3 large green peppers, chopped
- 1 cup olive oil
- 1 cup diced ham
- 3 bay leaves
- 1 cup red wine vinegar
- salt as needed

Clean beans, Wash in a colander very carefully to remove any dirt. Soak the beans overnight. To begin cooking fry onion, garlic and green peppers in 1/2 cup olive oil until tender. Combine all: beans, the onion-pepper mixture, diced ham, bay leaves and water to cover. Cover; cook until beans are tender and liquid is thick. Then add any salt as needed, red wine vinegar and 1/2 cup olive oil. Serve this over boiled rice. Put chopped onions on top of black beans. Serves 6.

I prefer Mahatma yellow saffron rice.

Fried Rice

- 3 1/2 cups cooked regular rice, chilled
- 2 eggs, slightly beaten
- 1 cup cooked pork, ham, chicken or beef
- 1/4 cup diced green onion
- 1 8-oz. can water chestnuts, drained and sliced
- 1 8-oz. can sliced mushrooms, drained
- 3 Tbls melted margarine
- 2 Tbls light soy sauce
- 1/2 tsp sugar

Stir-fry rice, eggs, meat, onion, water chestnuts, and mushrooms in margarine. Stir constantly as mixture heats. Stir in soy sauce and sugar. Serve hot. Makes 4-6 servings

Colonial Corn Pie

- 1 #303 can whole kernel corn and liquid, save 1 Tbls corn for garnish
- 1 Tbls chopped parsley
- 1/3 cup evaporated milk
- 2 egg yolks
- 1 12-oz. package corn muffin mix
- 1 Tbls pimento
- 1 1/2 tsp onion salt
- 3-4 drops Tabasco sauce
- 2 egg whites stiffly beaten
- sliced or diced cooked turkey and gravy to cover bottom of casserole
- 2-3 whole pimentos for garnish

Combine all ingredients except egg whites in a mixing bowl. Stir, but not too much. The batter should be slightly lumpy. Gently fold in the stiffly beaten egg whites. Place a layer of sliced turkey in the bottom of a shallow buttered baking dish. Spoon batter into dish. Bake at 350 degrees about 30 minutes or until golden brown. Serve from baking dish with extra gravy if desired, the recipe makes 5-6 servings. For garnish cut poinsettia petals from whole canned pimento with scissors. Make center of corn kernels.

This makes a lovely holiday vegetable dish without the turkey or with the turkey as a main dish.

❦ Marci Griffin

Creamed Corn

- 20-oz. pkg frozen cream style corn (tube package)
- 1/4 cup skim milk
- 2 Tbls oleo

Wipe down a 7-inch iron skillet with olive oil. Mix thawed corn with milk and oleo. Cook at 325 degrees for about an hour stirring every 10 minutes.

❦ Juanita Krumnow

Minorcan Black-eyed Peas

- 24-oz. bag dried black-eyed peas
- 3 large smoked ham hocks
- 1 pkg boneless smoked ham hocks, diced
- 1 large onion, cubed
- 1/2 large green pepper, diced
- 1/2 tsp red pepper
- 1/2 tsp black pepper
- 1/2 tsp oregano
- 1/2 tsp diced garlic in oil
- 1 Tbls Tabasco sauce
- 1 dash vinegar
- 3 large dried bay leaves

Combine ingredients in large pot. Cover with water, bring to rapid boil, reduce heat. Check water level in hour or so and add water if needed. Simmer a minimum of four hours.

❦ Joseph B. Griffin, III (Skip)

Cheese Garlic Grits

• 1 cup grits
• 1 cup strong cheese
• 1 clove garlic, pressed

Cook grits according to package directions. When done, stir in finely cut or grated cheese. Stir in garlic, salt and pepper to taste. Serves 4-6.

If you have leftovers pack in a refrigerator dish and chill it. Slice it, making slices a little less that an inch thick, dip the slices in beaten egg and then in flour. Fry in butter until brown.

Garlic Cheese Grits

For a large group.

• 3 1/2 qts water
• 1 1/2 Tbls salt
• 4 cups uncooked regular grits
• 5 garlic cloves, minced
• 1 2-lb loaf Velveeta cheese, cubed
• 1 cup half-and-half
• 2/3 cup butter or margarine

Bring water and salt to a boil in a large Dutch oven; gradually stir in grits and garlic. Cover, reduce heat, and simmer, stirring occasionally, for 10 minutes Add cheese, half and half and butter; simmer, stirring constantly, until cheese and butter melt. Serves 36.

Hopping John

Black-eyed Peas

- 3/4 cup chopped onion
- 1/2 cup chopped celery
- 1 tsp olive oil
- 2 16-oz. cans ready-to-serve reduced sodium, fat-free chicken broth
- 1/2 cup wild rice, uncooked
- 1 cup frozen blackeyed peas
- 1/2 cup long grain rice, uncooked
- 3/4 cup chopped tomato
- 2 tsp lemon juice
- 2 Tbls chopped fresh parsley
- 1/2 tsp salt
- 1/4 tsp red pepper

Cook onion and celery in olive oil in a large saucepan over medium heat, stirring constantly, until tender. Add Chicken broth; bring to a boil. Wash wild rice in 3 changes of hot water; drain. Add wild rice to broth mixture. Cover, reduce heat, and cook 30 minutes. Add black eyed peas and next 7 ingredients; cover and cook 20 minutes or until rice is tender. Makes 4 servings

Jalapeño Sauce
- 3/4 cup plain nonfat yogurt
- 1 clove garlic, minced
- 1/4 cup seeded and chopped jalapeño peppers
- 1/4 cup chopped fresh cilantro
- 1 tsp frozen unsweetened orange juice concentrate, thawed
- 1/2 tsp ground cumin
- 1/4 tsp salt

Combine all ingredients. Makes 1 cup.

Marinated Tomatoes

- 2 large tomatoes
- 1 large Vidalia or Texas 1101 onion
- 1/4 cup wine vinegar
- 3 tsp sugar
- 3 tsp basil
- 1 tsp tarragon
- 1 pinch oregano
- salt and pepper to taste
- 1/4 cup olive oil

Slice tomatoes and cover with a layer of sliced onion. In a separate bowl, combine the vinegar, sugar and seasonings; then mix the olive oil in well to make a smooth dressing. Now drizzle 1 to 2 tablespoons of this mixture over the sliced onions and tomatoes. Start all over again with the remaining tomatoes, onions and dressing and keep repeating until you run out. Refrigerate before serving. Serves 2.

Marinated Carrots

- 2 lbs sliced carrots
- 1 medium onion
- 1 bell pepper
- 1 cup sugar
- 3/4 cup cider vinegar
- 1/2 cup Wesson oil
- 1 can tomato soup
- 1 tsp dry mustard
- 1 tsp Worcestershire sauce
- 1 tsp slat and black pepper to taste

Cook carrots until tender. Add onion and bell pepper and bring to a boil. Remove from heat and let stand a few minutes covered in refrigerator. Serve warm.

🍴 Juanita Krumnow

Margarine Covers the Bread

In the Fall, after a weekend at home, my freshman in college daughter, Emily, was about to leave to go back to the university only to find that her little blue Mustang had a dead battery.

One of the reasons I had moved back to Montgomery was because I was rearing three daughters by myself and if I needed some muscles to flex behind me, I had Daddy there to fit the bill. Everybody loved him but *nobody* dared cross him except my little one Claire. Often times, when he was huffing and puffing and about to blow, she would lean over, pat him on the leg, and say, "Oh Grand Daddy, you don't mean that." It usually shocked him so, he melted. Daddy was retired and had owned a marine store in Montgomery for 40 years and still had all kinds of odds and ends left over and stored. I think we could safely call him a miser.

At any rate, I called him that morning to get some help. He arrived with frost blowing out of his mouth, yanked open the hood of the car and got to work. In about fifteen minutes he came in and said she was ready to go. We all walked out to admire his handiwork. There was the little Mustang purring like a kitten. We all let out a collective gasp. The car was running all right but it looked awful. The hood was sticking up about eight inches and there was a long narrow piece of carpet hanging out on both sides of the car. The hood was tied down with an old piece of rope. He had replaced the dead battery with a marine battery. Now, a marine battery is about twice the size of a car battery but that had been no problem to Daddy. All the cables were hooked up, the battery was sitting on top of the space a normal battery fit into, and it was running.

I thought to myself: "Margarine covers the bread but it ain't butter."

I shot a quick 'Mother Look' at Emily that said if you open your mouth or start crying you've had it. Emily got in the car and the last we saw of her, as she drove away, was the carpet flapping against the car. It looked more like a car driving itself down the street. You could hardly see her head she was so slumped down behind the wheel. You can imagine how mortified she was to have to take that car back to school and drive it looking like that.

Daddy and I went in and had a nice cup of hot coffee.

I Corinthians 13: 4 — *Love is patient and kind; love is not jealous or boastful; it is not arrogant or rude. Love does not insist on its own way; it is not irritable or resentful.*

Mushrooms with Tomatoes

- pkg Portobello mushrooms
- 2 tomatoes, peeled and chopped
- 1 onion,chopped
- 1 Tbls olive oil
- 1 garlic clove, minced
- 5 basil leaves, chopped
- salt, pepper, and fresh marjoram if available

Wash and dry mushrooms. Sauté onion in olive oil, add mushrooms, tomatoes, garlic and spices. Cook about 5 minutes. Serve as a main course with saffron (yellow) rice. Sprinkle with balsamic vinegar.

Okra and Tomatoes

- 1 medium onion and green pepper, chopped
- 2 Tbls oil
- 4 cups sliced fresh okra
- 3 medium tomatoes, peeled and chopped
- 1 tsp sugar
- 3/4 tsp salt
- 1/4 tsp pepper

Sauté pepper and onion in oil until tender. Add okra, tomato and remainder of ingredients, Cover and simmer about 15-20 minutes until the vegetables are to your desired doneness. I prefer still firm.

❦ Marge Zupko

Potato Casserole

- 1 1/2 bags Ore-Ida potato O'Brien, slightly thawed in microwave
- 1 can cream of celery soup, low fat
- 1/2 cup low-fat sour cream
- 1/3 cup low-fat light cream cheese
- 1 cup shredded Nacho-taco cheese, Sargento
- paprika

Mix cream cheese, sour cream and soup together. Warm in microwave until melted. Chop onion in processor, cook in microwave about 15 seconds. Add to cheese-soup mixture. Layer bottom of pan with potatoes, sauce, potatoes, sauce, then sprinkle with cheese, add paprika on top. Bake at 400 degrees for 30-45 minutes.

🌹 Juanita Krumnow

Rutabagas

- 2 small to medium rutabagas, peeled
- small piece of fat back
- 1 tsp sugar
- salt and pepper to taste

Bring fat back and water to a boil and simmer about 15 minutes. Peel rutabagas, add other ingredients and simmer until tender. Drain water, mash and add 2 teaspoons of butter and salt and pepper to taste.

Rustic Rutabagas

- 2 cups cooked seasoned rutabagas
- 2 Tbls flour
- 1 egg

Mash rutabagas, stir in flour and egg. Shape in patties; brown in butter and oil. Top with cheese sauce or grated cheese to serve.

Turnip Greens
with Pot Liquor Dumplings

- 2 lbs fresh young turnip greens, with roots if desired
- 1/4 lb salt pork or desired amount bacon drippings
- salt to taste
- enough water to have 3 cups liquid when done
- dumplings, or pot dodgers (see below)

To clean and wash greens, put picked greens in cold water in the sink and sprinkle with salt. In a 3-quart saucepan combine salt pork, salt and water. Cover pan and bring to simmering. Add washed greens, cover, and cook gently until greens are tender. Add peeled, chopped roots. Arrange dumplings as desired on dish with greens.

Dumplings
We call these pot dodgers

- 1 cup cornmeal
- 1/2 tsp salt
- 2/3 cup boiling water
- pot liquor

Combine cornmeal and salt in a mixing bowl. Stir boiling water into cornmeal mixture and stir to blend well. Using a heaping tablespoon for each portion, shape into balls and place gently in boiling hot liquid from cooked greens. Replace cover, simmer slowly until dumplings are done, about 20-30 minutes. Remove from heat and let stand 10 minutes.

Squash Casserole

- 12-15 medium yellow squash
- 10-12 saltines, crushed
- 3/4 stick butter
- 2 medium onions
- 2 eggs, beaten
- 2 small cans evaporated milk
- salt and pepper to taste

Slice squash and onions. Cook in unsalted water until done, about 20 minutes. Taste for salt. Drain well-add butter and saltines. Mash with potato masher. Add beaten eggs, milk and white pepper to taste. Mix well. Pour into greased 3-quart casserole. Bake at 350 degrees for about 30 minutes. Put grated cheese on top before done. To be done, it should be settled (not milky) and a little brown around edges.

❦ Billie Creech Horne

Sour Cream-Horseradish Sauce For Vegetables

- 1 8-oz. carton of sour cream
- 3 Tbls horseradish
- 2 Tbls peanut butter, crunchy or smooth
- 1/2 tsp salt

Mix together and refrigerate for several hours. Use as a sauce for any strong vegetable ie. asparagus, cauliflower, broccoli.

If you would like additional copies of *Angels in the Kitchen,* send $12.95 plus $3 to cover cost, postage and handling to:

Angels
P.O. Box 235
Kingsbury, TX 78638

Phone: 830-639-4244
E-mail: revpbk@axs4u.net

☛ Make checks payable to Patti Brooks Krumnow.

Enclose a note on how you would like your book inscribed, and I will personally autograph a copy for you — Patti

Printed on Recycled Paper

Index

Index

Index

Index

Index

Index

If you would like additional copies of *Angels in the Kitchen*, send $12.95 plus $3 to cover cost, postage and handling to:

Angels
P.O. Box 235
Kingsbury, TX 78638

Phone: 830-639-4244
E-mail: revpbk@axs4u.net
Web page: http://www.hillcountrysun.com/angel/angel.html
☞ Make checks payable to Patti Brooks Krumnow.

Enclose a note on how you would like your book inscribed, and I will personally autograph a copy for you — Patti

Printed on Recycled Paper